THE OPPOSITE OF POVERTY IS FRIENDSHIP

You're Richer Than You Think

DURAN PRICE

DEDICATION

Dedicated to Shakrista, in honor of your dad, Stephen. I have been blessed immeasurably by his friendship and miss his short, infectious bursts of laughter.

"The greatest good you can do for another is not just share your riches, but to reveal to him his own."

~ **Benjamin Disraeli**

CONTENTS

PREFACE

Friends are God's way of taking care of us.
~ **Author Unknown**

You're not going to believe this. The biggest fans of this book now were not initially excited when I first told them I was going to write a book about friendship. This is precisely why I knew I had to write it and why I'm so happy you are reading it. Just like the air we breathe, the water we drink, and the friends we have, we take for granted the things in life that sustain us most. We are blind to what is in front of us and only notice it when it's gone.

I wrote The Opposite of Poverty Is Friendship hoping it would do exactly what it seems to be doing: giving people a moment to pause and reflect on the blessings of their wonderful friendships, and to reach out to let friends know how much we really appreciate having them in our lives.

I share with you my personal stories of friendships through love and murder, laughter and turmoil, homelessness and hope, brotherhood and brawls, wisdom and redemption and the greatest treasures known to man. My hope is that through these stories you may see your own. I hope they act as a mirror and inspire personal reflection so you can see the immense value of the friends you have been gifted. And I hope you will let them know!

Writing this book took a hundred years longer and

was a thousand times harder than I thought it would be. But if it encourages you to recognize the treasured friendships in your life and motivates you to honor them in some small way, it will be worth every drop of blood, sweat and tears.

Thank you for reading.

ACKNOWLEDGMENTS

I am grateful for the fans I have received since writing this book. I would like to especially thank my first draft reviewers: you helped me in so many immeasurable ways. Thank you for taking the time to read the manuscript and for providing me with honest and useful feedback.

I appreciate your shared excitement, encouragement and insight that helped me to make this book better. I will be forever grateful to:

Dion, Marina, Wayne
Roper, Charlotte, Acolla
Felicity, Joe

To my editor John Harten
To my wife Juliana
And, of course, to ALL of my friends.
You make my life's journey easier.

1 A View To A Kill

I've learned that people will forget what you said, people will forget what you did, but people will never forget how you made them feel.
~**Maya Angelou**

Twice on Saturday April 13, 2013, my heart would explode in my chest, though I wouldn't fully understand why until the next morning. The first time it happened, I was watching a Colombian TV series called *Pablo Escobar, The Boss of Evil*. In a heart-wrenching scene, Fabio, one of Pablo's closest childhood friends, was brutally shot and killed in front of him.

From the beginning of the series, even before Pablo married Fabio's sister, you could tell they were as close as Saturday is to Sunday. The crackling sound of the bullets that punctured Fabio's body shredded Pablo's heart and brought him to his knees, weeping inconsolably. My chest almost collapsed under the weight of that scene. I could feel their closeness and the loss. Tears ran down my cheek as I blinked to run away from that feeling. I had no idea the same thing was happening to me 1200 miles away.

In an attempt to escape the pain after what I had just seen, I switched to another TV program called *Breaking Bad*. Unbelievably, I would witness an identical scene unfold. The character Gus Fring would watch in tortuous pain as his close friend was gunned down while trying to save Gus' life. From the moment the gunfire began and the first bullet hit this man who was like a brother to him, I was paralyzed. In slow motion, the camera showed Gus' grief, heartbreak and desperation in his desire to "unmake" the moment that was unfolding in front of him. Gus was a hard man, but this broke him. He wailed inconsolably.

In that moment my heart broke, as I imagined it was my best friend or brother. It was painful to watch. Images passed through my head about the possibility of this ever happening to me, and my mind short-circuited at the thought. I couldn't process it. Yet several hours later, on Sunday, I was forced to.

I woke up on Sunday morning to a text message from Dwayne, one of my closest friends and the big brother I never had. He said it was urgent so I called. He said, "I guess you didn't hear?" I knew from that point this couldn't be good as the delay was obviously his way of preparing me for what was to come next. "Steve's dead. He was murdered last night."

Stephen and I shared an unbreakable bond of friendship for twenty years and I loved him dearly. He was stabbed in the heart that Saturday night and pronounced dead at the hospital. I hung up the phone. Like a swollen grape severed from its vine, my heart fell, beyond my feet, through the floor, and into a dark hole in the earth beneath me. I sobbed buckets.

Connected by the same umbilical cord, our mutual love and respect could not be measured by man-made instruments. As a young kid, he took me under his wing. Steve taught me how to drive a standard shift car. I practiced in his shiny Volkswagen Jetta though I had no insurance or means to pay him back if I wrecked it. We shared a love for spirituality, a good laugh, and more than once fell for the same woman, a dual testament of trust and taste.

In the last conversation we would ever have, Steve asked when I would be back in The Bahamas because he wanted me to meet his estranged daughter. He hoped she could learn a little more about him through our friendship. I felt honored. At the time, I was 1200 miles away. On my next trip to The Bahamas I tried unsuccessfully to meet up with him before returning to Canada. How could I have known that a week later he would be taken from me, taken from his family, taken from this Earth? His passing is a loss I feel daily.

When I gave the eulogy at Stephen's funeral, I mentioned how he always made me feel special. I know now that this is one of the most important characteristics of a friendship or any type of relationship. Maya Angelou was right. I may not recall every single word or deed between us, but Steven Alexander Williams always made me feel special.

In his honor, I dedicate this book to the friendship we shared, and to the wonderful friendships I've been fortunate to have. They are a genuine treasure and I encourage you to acknowledge the blessing of real friends while they are still with you.

2 Cars Make Terrible Soups

While I was in the hospital, my mortgage didn't visit me.
~ Bill Miller

I once asked a close friend if he had to choose between being genuinely liked in a community or having lots of money what he would choose. And like the heathen that he is, he chose the money! His reasoning was that you don't have to be liked if you have money, as people will do what you wish anyway. I'll keep praying for him.

In my experience, friendship trumps money any day of the week. Genuine friendship is the most important gift you will have in your entire life. Your true friend will bail you out of life or death situations, comfort you in the depths of despair, make moments great because they were there to share them with you, and be a constant source of support throughout your lifetime. They will shower you with countless gifts you could not buy, not even with all the money in the world. And you will do the same for them.

William Miller was a great human being and a man among men. He had a tremendous heart, and always put the needs of others above his. He rejoiced in other people's joy and always tried to do the right things for the right reasons. William also happened to be a preacher. He wasn't a good man because he was a preacher; he was a good preacher because he was good man. Sadly, he passed away this year after a long fight with cancer. He was a genuine friend to many. Even throughout his tough and unbearable battle with cancer, he still found time to encourage as many as would let him. As he reflected on his time in the hospital and the pain and loneliness one feels, he had this to say:

While I was in the hospital, my mortgage didn't come to visit me. My car didn't cook me soup and my bank account didn't rub me down. My TV didn't check on me and my possessions didn't pray for me. Only my friends did that!

Pause and think of the genuine, beautiful friendships you have been blessed with. You are fortunate to have them in your life, some for a season and others for a lifetime. They represent gifts great and small that make this journey all the more bearable, all the more wonderful.

Stop to recognize them. Acknowledge and thank them for being a friend. Thank them for their acts of kindness. Thank them for choosing you and coming to your rescue repeatedly without expectation of reward.

Our friends love and care for us. They want the best for us and ask nothing in return. It would be a sin to take such a gift for granted. You are blessed to have them in your life, and if you are really lucky, they are blessed to have you in theirs.

3 It Takes One To Get One

The only reward of virtue is virtue; the only way to have a friend is to be one.
~ Ralph Waldo Emerson

On occasion, I hear people lament that they don't have any friends or that the ones they have sometimes mistreat them. My advice here is simple; the best way to gain a friend is to be one, but choose your friends wisely.

My friend Peter was born four years after World War I and retired before portable cell phones were invented. Despite using a walker on long walks, he lives alone and has two cars. Yes he still drives! We met at a Toastmaster's meeting a few years ago and I helped him to his seat. When the meeting was over I walked him to his car and we talked for a bit.

Peter told me of his wife Cynthia's passing a few months before and how hard it had been. They were married longer than I'd been alive. After I put his walker in the back, he got into the front seat of his minivan, thanked me for walking him to his car and buckled up. Then off he went like Christopher Lloyd in *Back to The Future*, only slower. Much slower.

Since then I've taken an interest in his well-being and enjoy talking to him. He's the consummate gentleman, sharp, witty and tells stories like a modern-day Dickens. Peter also calls frequently to check in on me and we've become good friends. He often tells me how he really appreciates when I get a chance to walk him to his car or call to check on him.

I naturally took an interest in Peter and his well-being without thinking about anything in return. However, what I got was a genuine friend that would do anything in his power to help me out if I ever needed it. Be a friend and take a genuine interest in someone. The rest naturally falls into place.

If you feel like you don't have any friends, ask yourself if you are being a good friend. You may not be. This is what Colombians call "sin anestesia!" or "without an anesthetic." It may come across as a painful blow with nothing to soften it. To be clear, this book is not about how to gain lots of casual friends or manipulate people into doing what you want them to do. There are tons of books out there that talk about that, but I usually ignore them because friendship should be genuine. It's not about what you can get; it's about what you can give and the joy of sharing.

If that seems harsh, it is not my intention to offend. Genuine friendships are not something that you can purchase or deserve. It's more like grace; undeserved and unearned favor and kindness. The best analogy for grace I ever read came from a web posting I got from my good friend Felicity.

"I like to compare God's love to the sunrise. That sun shows up every morning, no matter how bad you've been the night before. It shines without judgment. It never withholds. It warms the sinners, the saints, the druggies, the cheerleaders—the saved and the heathens alike. You can hide from the sun, but it won't take that personally. It'll never, ever punish you for hiding. You can stay in the dark for years or decades, and when you finally step outside, it'll be there. It was there the whole time, shining and shining. It'll still be there, steady and bright as ever, just waiting for you to notice, to come out, to be warmed."

~ Glennon Doyle Melton

This is a beautiful analogy for friendship. Good friends are there for us no matter what. In rain or shine, whether we are feeling great or beige, whether we call them everyday or once a year, whether we buy them a birthday present or not, they are faithful like the sun, warming us always and seeking nothing in return.

While I know many people and have acquaintances I respect, I only have a few friends and even fewer really close ones. I think that's the way it is with most people. In fact I have more fingers than close genuine friends. It doesn't mean that the other people are treacherous, just simply that I've been blessed to have a few really good ones close to me and they have been more than enough.

If you feel you don't have any genuine friends, first make sure you are not taking the friends you have for granted. Many people believe they "deserve" it when friends lend them money, pick them up from work or call them out of the blue just to check on them.

You may not understand how blessed you are to have someone willing to do these things for you, selflessly. Perhaps you don't recognize the treasure in your pocket. Your treasure is not in the quantity but rather the quality of your friendships. It's not about the number of friends you can count; it's about the number of friends you can count on.

Steve Jobs, cofounder of Apple Computer once said, "At Apple we are as proud of the things we do as we are of what we don't do." This is a good rule to have with friendships as well. Be as proud of the friends you have as the ones you choose not to have.

One really great attribute of a true friend is that they recognize it is a blessing to have you as a friend. If they only seem to care about you when you have something to offer, my advice would be to keep such a person at arm's length or even consider not having them in your life at all. Don't commit to people that have demonstrated through their actions that they are not deserving or appreciative of your friendship.

Two reggae songs come to mind that crystallize this idea.

In the infectious reggae song *Love Life*, aka "Strange Things Are Happening," Little Howie laments:

> *"When mi have me money, seh mi have whole heap a friend,*
> *a mi seh when me money done a dem nah no mi again!*
> *'standin like Daniel in the lion's den!"*

And if you flunked Jamaican patois in high school, the song basically says when I had a lot of money, I had a lot of friends, but when my money disappeared, so did my so-called friends.

And Damian, son of the legendary Bob Marley put it this way:

"Use cheddar as a bait and you'll recruit a rat!"

"Cheddar" is often used in urban speak to refer to money and the singer cautions if you use money to attract friends, beware, because cheese only attracts rats, so this is the type of person you will attract.

Unlike the online world of Facebook where the focus is on quantity of friends, in the real world your focus should be on the quality of friends you have. The right types of friends are not interested in your material possessions or what you can do for them. They love and respect you for who you are. The wrong type of friends will use you for what you have and will cause more harm than good.

If you want to have good friends in life, be a good friend and choose your friends wisely. Pay attention to what's important to them. Be willing to listen and empathize and to demonstrate that you care about the things that matter to them. Genuine persons appreciate this and will respond in kind.

4 Wing Menders

A true friend knows your weaknesses but shows you your strengths; feels your fears but fortifies your faith; sees your anxieties but frees your spirit; recognizes your disabilities but emphasizes your possibilities.
~**William Arthur Ward**

Why are friendships so valuable?

President Ronald Reagan once said that even if he was attending a party with thousands of people, his wife Nancy could make him feel lonely just by leaving the room. Mother Teresa believed the most terrible poverty is loneliness and the feeling of being unloved.

We've all had encounters with loneliness and despair. Maybe it was the moment you got fired. Maybe you found out the person you loved was sleeping with someone else. Or maybe, despite your best efforts, life keeps kicking you and kicking you. But that's not the worst feeling in the world.

The absolute worse feeling in the world is after being beaten, arrested and imprisoned by life's hardships, you are given the chance to make one phone call to someone who cares but you can't think of a single soul.

Despite a world bursting with people, you cannot think of one person who understands your pain or can comfort you, so you return the phone to the warden without dialing a digit. Take a moment and imagine the enormity of that feeling. That, my friend, is the worst feeling in the world.

I remember having such a feeling while I was still in high school. It's tough being a teenager without a dollar in your pocket. Without a job, you have to ask for everything. This can be a humbling and sometimes humiliating experience. Even if you wanted to catch a bus to a movie or invite a girl out for ice cream you couldn't. Well, I couldn't.

But every other week while attending my church youth group, my friend Brian would walk by me and offer a handshake or a high-five. When I took his hand, it often had a $20 bill folded in the center of his palm. Just like that, he would give me twenty bucks. Quietly, discreetly, without expecting anything in return.

He might whisper, "I know how it is being in school and all bro" or something to that effect. Billions of people in the world, thousands in my school and scores in my church group, yet Brian stopped to show me I wasn't alone, that he cared about what happened to me. Embedded in this act of kindness is the essence of friendship.

A few years ago, I got an email in the middle of the night from Martha (not her real name). Martha was a young, bright beautiful girl who spoke three languages and had a great sales job at an international company. This provided her with lots of opportunities to travel the world and buy nice things. She was really good at her job and made a lot of money for the company.

She had a job she loved and was building the home of her dreams and had all the amenities one could want in life. Things didn't come easy for her. She had a very hard life growing up, including physical abuse, but thankfully she survived that to build an independent life for herself and she treasured her independence. She was also very willing to help others, and while she didn't have many friends, she certainly had acquaintances because of her generosity.

Martha is very petite in stature but tenacious. She once told me of a time she was held up at gunpoint at an ATM. The robbers demanded cash and forced her to withdraw as much out of her account as the card would permit, which she did. After withdrawing the cash they demanded that she get in their car, as the money wasn't enough for them. Now they wanted to take what no woman should be forced to give.

With a gun pointed directly at her head, she refused. She screamed and declared, "If you are trying to rape me, you had better kill me now because I will never permit that. I will never survive that. Kill me now!" Surprised that the little woman who was so frightened earlier at the ATM had now drawn a line beyond which she would not cross, even if it meant her death, they sped off. The men left her to find her way to safety after such a horrible ordeal. She was tough.

But in the email she sent me that Sunday night, she was anything but. She gave me a number to a hotel where she was staying and asked me to call her. Martha explained that since I had last seen her she had lost everything. She lost her job, her savings and the place she was renting. She had used the last bit of money she had looking for a job and spending a few nights in a hotel as she had nowhere to go.

She was using her laptop computer in the hotel lobby and was trying to find a buyer for it so she could get something to eat and pay for her hotel stay. Martha had already overstayed her time in the hotel by a few nights. She could not afford to pay, and now the hotel was demanding that she pay everything immediately or she would be kicked out and they would call the police. She pleaded with me to lend her a few dollars to get back on her feet and she would repay me as soon as she was able.

If you knew Martha, you would know that having to reach out to me in this way was one of the hardest things she ever had to do. She always took care of herself and she didn't want to have to depend on anyone for anything. She had already tried reaching out to people she had helped before. A girl at the office she loaned money to, another she roomed with before and a woman she helped to restore a wretched floor in her apartment. Each was too busy with their own lives to be bothered, she said. Knowing Martha, she probably retreated at the first sign they were unwilling to help.

To make things worse, at that time I was broke. Then again, if she had called at any other time, I probably would have still been broke. Don't judge me! But I had to do something. Martha was barely surviving on crackers and water for the past few days.

But more concerning than the emptiness of her purse was the hollow in her voice. Like a pelican stuck in the black thickness of an oil spill, each flap of her wings was weaker, more ominous than the one before it.

There is nothing more heartbreaking than a human being who's lost hope. It wasn't just the hope of finding a job or getting a dollar; she had lost hope in her fellow man. Seven billion people in the world, more than 120 million of them in her country, yet she felt she had no one. Then, at the intersection of desperation and despair, she called me. I was that last flicker from a cigarette lighter in shaky hands, thirty degrees below zero. I had to do something.

We didn't live in the same country, so physically going to her rescue was out. My bank account looked like hers, so that was out too. But I had friends. And I called on them. I called one of my friends and asked to borrow his credit card to pay a hotel bill, which he graciously said yes to without hesitation. Then I called another and borrowed money to send her so she could buy something to eat and have a few dollars for the week.

But before any of this, I told Martha: "Hey, listen to me, I don't have it, but I will make sure you get it and we will deal with this together. We will do whatever it takes for you to be okay and you will be okay. Tough times don't last, but tough people do and we will take care of this together."

For the rest of the week we would take care of the most necessary things. The hotel bill, affordable food. I convinced her to keep her laptop so she could search for a job. We found a nice old lady that had a room for rent. The lady added a small fridge to the room, a mattress and even waived the security deposit. Despite her previous life of means, Martha wasn't picky at all. She was grateful for everything she had. Each night we would talk. Each night she would cry.

Martha was broken by what had happened to her and felt alone. But that sadness soon turned to gratitude. She was so grateful for me calling and talking to her for hours and listening to her and encouraging her. Out of all the things I was able to provide for my friend, the one thing she said she treasured was that I brought her hope. Her faith was restored. She appreciated all the other things, but hope and the notion that someone cared was what she was most grateful for.

Less than two months later, she landed a job in Germany, all expenses paid, and she was off again. Just like that. She called me at the end of the first month on the job, updated me on things and asked for my bank details so she could return the money she had borrowed. I was so happy to hear that her spirit and the wings of her soul were restored. I asked her not to return the funds to me but to pay it forward by finding someone in need and helping them out. She agreed.

So, why are friendships so valuable? The very DNA of friendship can be clearly seen in a phrase made popular by one of the most famous stories of friendship, *The Three Musketeers*. Their motto "One for all and all for one" captures the beauty and value of friendship. If you're in need, I'll be there for you and I know you will be there for me whenever I'm in need. We'll take care of each other. How unbelievably cool is that?

5 The Psychologist, The Confidant, The Banker

As long as I owe you, you will never be broke!

When Juliet says, "A rose by any other name would smell as sweet" in *Romeo and Juliet*, she argues that what really matters is what something *is*, not what we call it. If I take advice about money from my next door neighbor, then he's my financial advisor. And although I may use the exquisite-sounding French word "escargot" while dining, it will still be a snail that I'm eating. Marketers use "fractional ownership" when referring to multiple persons sharing a condo they bought, but we know that's just a fancy term for timeshare. What matters is what is, not what we call it.

Is the tight-fitting red dress with the revealing split a perfect choice for the Christmas party? Ask Gina, your fashion designer. Can you afford to buy said red dress considering your current budgetary constraints? This is a question for April, your financial advisor. Will your ex,

Todd, be there with his new girlfriend? Matt, your private investigator, has you covered. Should you find a hot date to go with you to make your ex jealous? Should you even care? Relationship guru and part time psychologist Marissa springs into action. We may not use fancy terms to describe the roles friends play in our lives, but what matters is that they do and we are blessed to have them.

I remember going through a really rough period emotionally. I was trying to make sense of an important relationship that had ended badly and I was sad and depressed. I felt like I couldn't talk to anyone. I had good friends who truly cared about me, but felt like no one could relate to my growing pain and frustration. The hurt and sadness grew and I felt I was about to burst. I thought, *who in the world can I really talk to about this? This is not healthy and I need help*. Dr. Phil was out of the question. Then it hit me: I knew exactly who to call.

She was the one person in the whole world I felt at that moment would allow me to connect and release this burden that I carried. She could help me carry the load just by listening. Sort of like Michael Clarke Duncan in *The Green Mile*, but more gorgeous, and with much longer hair. I hadn't spoken to her for some time. So I called her up, pretending I was just calling about the weather, and then I burst.

A tsunami of tears, frustration, and pain left me in that moment. She was, as always, my angel, my psychiatrist, my confidant, my energy that simply reflected back that it was okay. Everything would be alright and I would be fine. She didn't actually say any of that. She just listened.

She didn't judge, she didn't become fearful, she didn't feel pressured to offer platitudinal advice. She just listened. I knew she loved me and was in my corner. In her quiet but unbreakable love and understanding, she reassured me that I would be okay and that this too shall pass. Even if I get Alzheimer's, it will be the one moment in life I will always remember and love her for.

On another occasion I remember chatting with my friend Keith. I was complaining about how someone I cared about really wronged me and how unfair it was. I started to plead my case to him as if he were a judge and I was looking for sympathy and justice. As I was about to kick it in high gear and show him just how slimy this person was, he cut me off. "Hey, they persecuted Jesus, and hung him on a cross, and *he* didn't do anything wrong!" Whack!

With the wisdom of king Solomon and the force of crashing into a mountain, he stopped me dead in my complaining tracks. He made me understand that as long as you are living, there will be people willing to wrong you, mostly through no fault of your own. Therefore, recognize this and don't beat yourself up over it. Release that burden and move on. While some people may refer to this as sage advice from a Zen master, I consider it just another day with my friend Keith, another remarkable day and I was glad to be in his company.

They say friends and money don't mix. Oil and water and all that. But I have a unique relationship with a special friend where we serve as each other's banker. It doesn't matter if it's $5 or $5,000. We approach each other with the confidence that if one person needs it, the other person will provide it. If the other person doesn't have it, they will find it. And we return it with mutual respect for the friendship and the value of how this helps make our lives a little easier. It's like we're on this journey up the Himalayas with one oxygen mask. We take turns passing it to each other so we both can survive. It's a beautiful thing and I marvel at it always.

My friend Kimwood once told me that he loaned a large sum of money to a friend that wasn't able to pay it back on time as promised. Kimwood said that this friend never tried to avoid him. He just told him that things didn't go according to plan and as a result he didn't have all the money owned. What was interesting however was that this friend told him, "But listen, if there is ever anything you need, anything at all, even a portion of what I owe you, just let me know and I will move heaven and earth to make that happen, because as long as I owe you, you will never be broke!"

That phrase stood out to me: "As long as I owe you, you will never be broke!" What he meant was that he considered Kimwood to be a true friend and that he would always be willing to do whatever he could in life for a true friend, and that was priceless. Listening to him recount that story, I recognized what true riches were and what true poverty was.

Money may come and go. Those who are driving nice cars today may find themselves on foot tomorrow. Life is like that. But true poverty is a man without real friends. Even if you happen to have money, if people visit you on your birthday, they do so for the food and wine. If they call you, it's to further their own cause. They don't care about you at all.

But a man with genuine friends always has someone to comfort him. He has scores of homes that welcome him and many families to dine with, all people who care for his well-being. Anything he needs, they will give him or help him to attain. If he is sick, they will care for him. If he is in danger, they will come to his rescue. If he is happy, they will celebrate with him. If he is sad, they will console him. There is no end to their generosity as they are motivated by love. Whether he has money or not, this man is truly rich. The opposite of poverty is friendship and a man who has no genuine friends, even if he has money, is actually poor.

6 The Power Of Sharing The Experience

Doing business without advertising is like winking at a girl in the dark. You know what you're doing, but nobody else does!
~ Stuart Henderson Britt

The Olympics are where dreams go to live forever. It gives birth to extraordinary performances where people are united through shared experiences. It's a great metaphor of friendship and also the setting for our next story.

Imagine you're at the summer Olympics in Beijing. China is a long way from The Bahamas. The pub you're standing in front of holds 350,000 people, matching the total population of your country except everyone here speaks Mandarin. A few people from other countries are there, but no one you recognize. It's track and field day and everyone is gathered around the big screens.

Eight runners line up. One from The Bahamas, two from China, and five from other competing countries. The gun pops and they're off! Everyone in the pub is cheering on their countryman, especially China as the home country. But slowly the Bahamian runner seems to be edging out and has a chance to place. Your heart pounds and you squeeze your fist. Inside, you're saying, *Come on! Come on!* But you control your excitement.

You're conscious that you are alone. In an electric burst of energy, your countryman puts on the turbochargers and peels ahead of the other runners. He triumphantly reaches the finish line first and takes the gold in the race! You're ecstatic but reserved! The other people in the bar were happy to cheer on their guys, and those who didn't place are completely disappointed.

For the second and third place finishers, you see people jumping up and down in the pub and cheering. You? You're happy, but you're the only one in the pub from your country so your experience is greatly diminished.

Now, imagine that very same experience again. But this time when you walk into the pub, you spot a table with your country's flag and five Bahamians screaming, "Let's go!" The national colors on your t-shirt and cap make them notice you. They've never seen you before, but you feel an instant connection. They greet you with cheers and call, "Hey brother! Over here! Have a beer! The race starts in one minute!" You instantly feel relieved, welcomed and excited, even though these were complete strangers seconds ago. You immediately feed off their energy and you all scream in unison "Bahamas! Bahamas! Bahamas!"

People from other countries, especially the local

Chinese, are present in the pub and you are greatly outnumbered, but you don't care. The race takes place in the same way. But now the five of you are cheering and you can hear the others at the table say things like, "I think we're going to do it! Look at him go!" One person grabs your shoulder and squeezes it in excitement and anticipation. You hit the table with your fist. "Go! Go!" and then, victory! The Bahamian athlete crosses the finish line first! Your table erupts with cheers like a giant bottle of coke shaken fervently before opening.

Spectators from other countries look on in amazement and a bit of jealously. They all know that your team won. Everyone at your table looks at each other and screams and jumps up and down! Eyes open to double their size in amazement! "DID YOU SEE THAT!" You all give fast, stinging high-fives, hug each other and jump up and down in jubilance. "We did it! We killed em! We're the best! Gold, baby! Whoooa!"

You've all just shared an experience that has changed your lives forever. You're intrinsically connected now like the five rings of the Olympic games. You have history together. Things will never be the same. That moment was solidified in each of your minds and hearts and brought you instantly closer. It's something that you will all treasure forever and it increased the value of what you witnessed and experienced a million fold.

That is the difference between going through life alone and going through life with a friend by your side to share in the experience. It doesn't matter whether the experience is good, bad, ugly, triumphant, joyful or otherwise incredible. You could just be witnessing something funny happening or learning that a family member passed away. You could have just found out you're going to have a baby, going to get married, lost your job or got a new one.

The power of the experience lies in that magical moment when we recognize we are not alone. Our friends walk with us. Friendship is like a candle lit in a dark room so that two persons can witness something wonderful happening and look at each other knowing that they were able to share that moment, and it makes the experience special. That's the difference between having an experience on your own in the dark or lit up like an Olympic torch so you can share it with someone. It's the difference between having a friend and not.

7 Unreliable Unless Needed

Animals are reliable, many full of love, true in their affections, predictable in their actions, grateful and loyal. Difficult standards for people to live up to.
~**Alfred A. Montapert**

Some people think that having a true friend means that whenever you call, they should be ready, willing and able to respond to your every need, one hundred percent of the time. And if they aren't, then they must not be a true friend. I've disproved this many times in my relationships with friends.

My friend Dion is never punctual. I have a better chance of getting pregnant than Dion showing up on time. It might be because he speaks Spanish and I just didn't know it. The Spanish word for "now" is "ahora," which can mean either "right now" or "soon/eventually." When Dion says "now" he usually means "eventually." Sure, he'll swing by. Maybe not at the agreed time, or day, or year, but "eventually" he will.

So, should I Donald Trump that relationship and give him the "you're fired" papers? Not a chance. I respect him immensely and he's one of my closest friends on the planet. I can forgive Dion's notion that time is a vague suggestion instead of a tool of precision. That's because he has another character trait that is far more valuable to me. He may not always be on time, but he's there when it matters most. He may let you down when you want him to be around, but he will definitely be there when you need him to be around.

I remember a scene in the movie *Mr. & Mrs. Smith* where Vince Vaughn's character gets an early morning call and he responds, "Tempting, but I don't get out of bed for less than half a million dollars." That's how Dion is. It's like he needs the game to be on the line to be excited enough to give the performance of his life. And wouldn't you want your best player, even if he performs horribly in the first quarter, to perform his best when the game is on the line?

I can remember asking this dude for $20 and he'd be like, "Sorry man, I don't have it, things are tough." Then, like two days later, I'd be working on an important business deal and I'd call him and go, "Listen I need $5000 dollars to close a big deal a.s.a.p." and he'd respond, "Ok, pick it up in the morning!" And sure enough, he'd have it or find it! I guess he just works better under pressure.

Having someone in your corner when you need them is much more important than having them around when you want them. With Dion, I have the assurance that if I need to talk at 3 a.m. or if my back is against the proverbial wall, he'd be there. In a crisis, he'd be like, "Hey, don't worry about it, we'll figure it out, and in the time needed." And I'll take that over someone who is only on time when my back is not against the wall any day of the week.

8 The Golden Mean

No one is perfect... that's why pencils have erasers.
~Author Unknown

In the philosophy of the golden mean, Aristotle argues that extreme views in anything can have negative consequences. Too much can be just as bad as too little, even in the pursuit of perfection. Like goldilocks and the three bears, sometimes the best porridge is not too hot or too cold, but just right depending on who's hungry.

I've gotten into a habit of making sure my car always has a crescent wrench, a Philips screwdriver and a butter knife. Having those three tools nearby has saved my life and that of friends and strangers on many occasions. Sometimes I use them to remove a car part or fix a loose doorknob, and more than once I've used my butter knife to help a neighbor locked out of her apartment. And no, I don't have any photos with a license plate on my chest! After every use I make sure to put them back in their place because I never know when I will need them again. And when I do, I'm always grateful that I valued them enough to keep them around.

Sometimes though, I have to use them for jobs that are ideally suited for another tool, like the time my car wouldn't start. My battery was as dead as a stag party without women or music. In the airport parking lot, a driver nearby offered to help. He didn't have jumper cables, but his car battery worked.

All I had to do was temporarily remove my battery, replace it with his to start my car, then put both batteries back. Ideally, the best tool for the job would be a ratchet with connectors for nuts and bolts of all sizes. A ratchet is great because it fits snugly and its long stem increases your reach in really tight spaces. The handle provides great torque so you don't need much strength to unscrew the nut. But I didn't have a ratchet. I only had my crescent wrench, which is bigger and more awkward to use in tight spaces.

This meant that I had to make fifty itty-bitty turns instead of a few quick and easy ones to remove the bolts that held the battery in place. At some point the nut at the bottom of the bolt would move freely as I tried to remove the bolt it was attached to. If I had pliers, I could keep the nut from moving. But I didn't have pliers, only my butter knife. I tried to find an ideal angle to place the knife so that the flat part of the blade could be pressed against the nut. This would keep the nut in place while I made tiny turns on the bolt with the crescent wrench until I could eventually access and remove the battery.

In this situation I had two choices. I could use my crescent wrench and butter knife to remove the dead battery, even though it would be a bit of a challenge. Or I could toss them to the side in frustration, forgetting all the times they came in handy I could instead pay a small fortune to call a wrecker to come for my car and a taxi to take me home. When you're cheap like me, the answer is simple. I got that dead battery out with the tools I had.

Really good friends are a lot like my favorite tools. They will always be there for you, save your life many times, and are invaluable. But sometimes they have shortcomings that become obvious when you have a particular kind of problem and that can be frustrating. Sometimes we're tempted to think that if this friendship cannot serve me in the way I want now, then perhaps I should trade it in for a "better" friendship.

That would be a mistake. Soon after switching friends, you will find yourself missing the experiences that made your first friendship special. You'll realize that changing friends is not like changing underwear, where any pair will do. Just like my crescent wrench and butter knife, your new friend may be great at some things but not so great at others.

Friends are not universally perfect; each has their benefits and flaws. You have built and maintained your friendships over the years for a reason. Your problem might be big, but don't make it bigger than it is, causing you to lose a precious ally.

Goethe wrote, "Certain flaws are necessary for the whole. It would seem strange if old friends lacked certain quirks."

My friend Steve was in many respects unreliable. This was specifically true if we ever arranged to meet on a certain date and time. He would be a no-show and would never call or even send a message saying he was not going to be able to make it. It would drive me nuts. Even worse were the excuses he would give for not being able to keep the appointment. He once gave the excuse that the reason he was six hours late for an appointment was that he forgot his belt! Like, Holy North Dakota!

Once I was hospitalized for two weeks because of a fast heartbeat and doctors were keeping me in for observation as they tried to figure out what was causing this. It would turn out that it was nothing more than a severe case of acid reflux because my eating habits were so poor. But until they found out, it was a really scary deal. Well, each day and often several times a day Steve would visit me in the hospital. He would constantly ask me if I needed anything. He would stay until the nurses on the ward would run him off so I could rest. I could set my watch by his visits. It's something that I appreciated and will never forget.

I felt the same way with Steve's friendship as I did with my trusty crescent wrench and butter knife. Despite being an awkward fit for tasks for which he was ill suited, Steve was perfect, valuable and indispensable for the things for which he was well suited. Insisting on perfection in everything often results in progress on nothing. This is the principle of the golden mean.

9 When $100 Becomes A Million

If you owe the bank $100, that's your problem. If you owe the bank $100 million, that's the bank's problem.
~J.P. Getty

The Three Amigos, starring Martin Short, Chevy Chase and Steve Martin, is one of the funniest movies ever made, because I said so. In one classic scene they were riding their horses into the desert for many miles without water, baked by the scorching sun, and were dying of thirst. Their pace was slow, their mouths were open, and they were sweating profusely. In desperation they stopped to see what water supplies they had left. Despite Chevy Chase's funny yet bad behavior, the scene is great because it shows that precious things like water are often only appreciated in scarcity.

Steve Martin was the first to open his water bottle and he raised it high above his head as he opened his mouth and leaned back to catch what little was left inside. A few drops trickled out and landed on his tongue. Martin Short was next, and when he tried to drink what he thought was water, a cascade of dirt gushed out of the canteen and into his mouth, almost choking him. I almost choked, with laughter.

Finally, Chevy Chase opened his canteen and a fountain of water flowed out into his mouth. It was such an abundance that he didn't even take care as to how much was directly going into his mouth versus on the side of his face and to the ground. Gulp, gulp! Hearing the sound of water glugging out, his friends, still weak from thirst, stared at him in amazement. He had so much water he began gargling and spitting it out, just for the fun of it. With jaws wide open in disbelief, Steve and Martin watched as Chevy wasted the precious commodity.

His next act had you bursting with laughter as he tossed his canteen to the ground. Still full of water, it spilled all over the hot, dry desert floor and immediately evaporated. His friends stared at him in disbelief and desperation. They were unable to speak because they were dying of thirst and because they were shocked by what they were seeing. Then, for an encore, Chevy takes out some lip balm and begins to liberally apply it to his lips. He then turns and sees his friends gawking at him in disbelief. Unaware of what they found so curious, he then puts his hand out in their direction and says, "Lip balm?"

Earlier in the movie, when these guys were back in their comfortable hotel suite, water was in abundance. Water was on the table, ice was in the fridge, showers were easy to come by. They never once thought about water as a precious or limited resource. They may have appreciated having a drink, but it was nothing compared to the desperation they would later feel riding in the hot desert and running out of water with hundreds of miles to go.

I had a similar experience with money and it taught me something. I borrowed a few grand from a friend for several weeks to help close a business deal. He provided the funds without thinking twice and while it was good for me to be able to move forward with my deal, I never felt the need to profusely thank him for it. We would lend this kind of money to each other at times so it didn't seem like a big deal when he lent it to me, even though I appreciated it.

Years later while walking downtown without two pennies to my name, I bumped into him. At the time, I was down on myself because I was an entrepreneur, working constantly, but had little to show for it. My ego was crushed, my resolve tested and I was fighting depression. On top of that, I hadn't eaten for the day and was starving. I was so desperate I probably would have done anything for a Happy Meal as long as there was a prize inside. Prizes are important!

I felt like Steve Martin and Martin Short wandering through the desert with no water. I needed to make an effort to get lunch but I was just emotionally and physically wrung out. I felt I had no options, which is the worst feeling in the world. I was just drained. After we exchanged pleasantries, I asked my friend if he had a few bucks on him. Without allowing me to finish my sentence, he goes into his pocket, whips out a crisp $100 bill and says, "This is all I have on me to spare right now, will that do?"

Just then, I felt the heavens open up and heard angels singing. That $100 bill felt like it came directly from heaven in the beak of a white dove just in the nick of time to save my life. It's an experience that has stayed with me. But not because of the money. I have both loaned and borrowed thousands of dollars from this friend before. So then, why was this $100 dollars so special? It was special because it came at time when I felt lonely, desolate and broken. I felt there was no one I could go to or wanted to approach. I had no hope.

You could lose every single thing in this world as a person and survive. You could lose your car, your house, your job, a loved one, your entire city. You could lose it all and survive and be okay. The one thing you can never ever lose and be okay is hope! Hope keeps us alive when we've lost everything. Hope is like a pulse or a heartbeat. As long as it's there, however faint, we know there's a chance and we feel the energy of that chance. It propels us forward.

The reason that day will always be special to me is not because my friend gave me a hundred bucks. It's because he gave me hope when I needed it and it mended my soul. He made me stop and acknowledge the power and blessing of a really good friendship. Though it was just $100 dollars, on that day it was more important than a few thousand dollars and in fact, it felt like a million!

10 Forgiveness And Wet Dollar Bills

Not forgiving is like drinking poison and expecting the other person to die.
~Anne Lamott

Everyone I love has pissed me off before. On many occasions, I'm sure I returned the favor. In fact, I wouldn't be surprised if the records show I gave as much as I got. We're human. It's inevitable. Even in the most heavenly of relationships, there will come a time, perhaps more than once, that your relationship is tested to see what it's made of. Far more important than the test itself is your reaction to it. Only a fool does not recognize the value of his possessions and so tosses them to the wind.

Have you ever accidentally left money in your clothes before doing the laundry only to find them soaking wet after the wash cycle? Imagine finding a wet hundred-dollar bill in the wash. Soaked and delicate, your first thought might be "Oh man, how could I have been so silly to do that?" followed by "It's ruined!" Then immediately followed by "Ruined my butt! That's a hundred bucks! I'll find a way to dry that baby out, it'll be ok eventually!" So you delicately remove it from the storm of being tumbled around with the clothes, you lay it on the counter or pin it to a hanger and then turn on the fan. After a while, it will dry, and you will rejoice like someone just gave you a hundred bucks. Your prodigal hundred was lost, but now it's found :)

Remember this when you have an argument with a friend that really tests your relationship because you were hurt or because you hurt them. Despite our human reaction to want to get even or write off the relationship because of pride or anger, that would be a mistake. Although your friendship appears to be all wet and beaten at that moment, it's still incredibly valuable and it can be saved. In fact, it's in our best interest to save a friendship because it will continue to benefit us the rest of our lives. Remove it from the turbulent situation, set it aside and give it time to dry and heal, then go back to it and recognize it for its value.

Ever since I was a little kid, I have been very protective of my privacy, my personal space and personal items. I also respect other people's privacy. As a young adult, ready to date and take on the world, I invited an attractive girl over to my apartment. She, however, invited herself into my bedroom. My antenna immediately went up, as I consider the bedroom to be a sacred place where people are only allowed when invited. I think I got that from my grandmother. I went to use the bathroom and when I returned to the bedroom, I found this girl going through my drawers!

She realized that I had come back into the room yet

proceeded to open other drawers and move clothes around as if searching for something. "Don't mind me, I like to search!" she quipped nonchalantly. I'm thinking to myself, "This succubus can't be serious!" I pulled her hand away from the drawer and said, "What the hell are you doing? I don't like people going through my stuff. You have to leave." She looked at me as if to say what's the big deal? The only thing I could think of was the famous line from comedian Janeane Garofalo: "Ok, pack it up people, you don't have to go home but you can't stay here!" I kicked her out and that was the last time I saw her.

I contrast this experience with one I had in high school. We always wanted to look our best. I kept several essential items in my knapsack at all times. These included a hairbrush to keep my sleek waves in order, and a shoe brush and polish so my Clarks would always be crisp. One day during recess I entered our homeroom and could see from a distance that my school bag had been unzipped and left open. I thought "What the…?" and my blood started to boil. All I could feel was the invasion of my personal space and violation.

Glancing to the corner of the room, I saw Sean, one of my best friends, with his foot on one of the chairs, stooped over and brushing away. The room started spinning. He turned to me and said, "Hey man, I borrowed your brush!" and without thinking I snatched it out of his hands like a lion snatching her cub from a predator's jaws. By this time my skin was turning red and burning, not an easy feat for a black dude. Smoke charged out of my ears, the anger built and I snapped. I called him words that even a writer of skanky porn would consider too dirty to publish.

Sean was taken aback by my reaction. We had been best of friends for so long and spent so much time together he just could not understand why I would have such a reaction to someone simply borrowing a shoe brush. He couldn't relate to my sense of violation. I could not get the imagery out of my head. My bag where I kept all of my personal items and secrets was snatched away, forced open by hands without consent. The perpetrator rummaged through my private things, searching for the one they wanted, and then tossed my school bag to the side, open and naked for the world to see. Poor Sean, I think he felt like he was in the Twilight Zone.

Right then and there, I decided that wasn't a friendship I wanted anymore. Anyone who could do such a thing was probably capable of violating goats. As far as I was concerned at that point, he most likely did, and I would have none of it. Screw that friendship. I didn't talk to Sean for weeks.

We were in the same class, would see each other daily and the sudden excommunication during those weeks would be difficult for both of us because we used to spend a lot of time together; talking, joking, laughing, riding bikes, gawking at the pretty girls in the school and of course, spending time with our first love, the computer. Sean made several attempts to mend the relationship at that point but I was still way too upset. I wanted him to suffer for what he did.

Then something strange happened. As more time

went by and I started spending time with my "substitute friends," I became painfully aware that it was not the same. They had no idea that a "bit" was a binary digit. The concept of sneaking into the library to read the research on sexual response by Masters & Johnson was otherworldly to them and I couldn't begin to explain what was interesting about it or other topics of human psychology.

Bike rides were now infinitely longer as there was no chatting, no adventure during the journey. As we unwisely do at times, I had tossed my water-damaged hundred-dollar bill aside, not recognizing its value. I still had two years left in high school and if I didn't want to have a significantly diminished experience, I had to learn an important lesson fast. I had to learn to forgive.

I looked for the opportunity to talk to Sean about it. My normal skin color returned and my ears were no longer setting off smoke alarms, so I was able to more calmly address the situation. I explained why this apparently simple act of borrowing a shoe brush without my consent was such a big deal to me. Sean apologized and said he understood how his actions could have been taken the wrong way even though we had a great friendship. Well, he said he understood. Sometimes I think he was just like, "This dude is goddamned crazy! I'm just gonna smoke the peace pipe before he really loses it." But either way, his apology was accepted.

I was fourteen at the time of that incident and Sean and I were very close back then. Since that time however, the experiences that we have shared and the depth of our friendship have dwarfed anything we had previously experienced. Somewhere between there and here, we became brothers, would stand as best man at each other's weddings, and provide incalculable support to each other through life's many experiences. If asked, I would not trade our friendship and shared experiences for a million dollars. Though my answer to that question would probably get fuzzy around the ten million dollar mark, but Sean would understand.

Forgiveness is the fan that allows us to cool off a soaked and temporarily damaged friendship so that it can heal and so that its value in our lives can be fully realized. You would be a fool not to forgive a true friend because it will primarily be your loss if you don't. Sean and I have had a million more arguments and a million more misunderstandings. But because we fully understand the value and the blessing of our friendship, we're always happy to sprinkle a bit of forgiveness whenever necessary. Our friendship is too valuable not to.

11 Use Baselines To Avoid Flatlines

Now, faith is the substance of things hoped for, the evidence of things not seen.
~ Hebrews 11:1

Where are you now? That's the first question we ask if someone gets lost on the way to our house and calls for directions. Why do we ask that question?

To solve any problem or know any truth, we need a baseline. We use what we know to help us understand what we don't. Remembering this important truth will serve you well in life. Ignoring it can cost you dearly.

The instructions to boil an egg might read; bring water to a boil, add egg, then let it cook for ten minutes. How long it takes the water to boil depends on a lot of factors. Maybe the water is ice cold. Maybe it's winter and the temperature is below zero. Or perhaps the fire on your stove is not that powerful.

Despite all these things, you rely on the one thing you

do know. When the water starts to bubble, it has come to a boil and you can now add the egg. Once again, you rely on your baseline, something that you do know to help you figure out what you do not know.

The same goes for a lighthouse or radar. These are perfect examples because we use them to guide us when there are strange and uncomfortable forces around us like darkness or fog that can confuse us. This confusion may scare us, cause us to act irrationally, or even capsize our boat.

So we rely on what we *do* know to help us navigate what has become scary, unfamiliar or concerning territory. This reliance on what we do know guides us to safety. Incidentally, this also encourages us to rely on our lighthouse with even more confidence in future because the experience is now a familiar one.

Lets go back to our first example where you were trying to help someone find directions to your house. You may ask your friend to tell you which street they are on and which direction they are heading in. You may also ask them if they have already passed a landmark, like the statue of the brown pigeon with two heads.

In all of these inquiries you are trying to establish a baseline for what is true. From that point it will be easy to guide your friend by saying, "Ok great, take the next left, third right and my house is the yellow one on the corner with the boat parked in the driveway." Without a baseline, directions would be impossible. But with a baseline, your friend's anxiousness about being lost will subside. They'll have information that will comfort and guide them when they are surrounded by otherwise unfamiliar and perhaps even uncomfortable territory.

Pay attention, because what follows is vital to the longevity of any meaningful friendship. If you understand this truth, you will avoid premature wars based on false or misleading information. You will save valuable friendships from casualties of this very real and often misunderstood human condition.

When there is doubt and confusion, rely on the reputation of a person to help you make sense of what is happening in time of trouble. This is their baseline and the baseline of your relationship with them.

Too often, we are willing to throw away ten years of data because a current situation or problem, taken in isolation, may suggest a misunderstood motive. While it may seem natural to only rely on the data in front of you, consider the wealth of historical data you have to provide context and to serve as your lighthouse.

Suppose you often lend money to a friend who has always paid on time in the last five years. But this time he hasn't. So you sit in silence, getting angrier day by day, as he has not paid you back nor said anything to you. Then you start talking to your other friends about it. You tell them how you are so disappointed in your friend who didn't have the decency to pay you back on time or at least say something.

On top of this you start to show an attitude with your friend without saying what is bothering you directly. You allow your friendship to erode because, as far as you're concerned, if he was a real friend he would pay on time and if he was an honorable person he would at least be able to come to you to say something about it. So you cut him off.

The problem with this fuzzy math is that you are not using the data of your entire friendship to guide you in understanding what could be going on at this point. Since he has always paid you back in the past and always on time, that is a much better indicator of the type of person he is than this current scenario because you have a lot more data there.

It also suggests that whatever is different this time is not the rule but rather an exception to the rule of how he governs himself. This in and of itself should be enough for you to regard what is happening now as a one-time thing. Most likely there is a good reason for this and you do not currently have all the facts.

Obviously, calmly talking to someone about an issue that concerns you is better than speculating in private and holding a hidden but growing malice in your heart. This is especially true when it involves someone that has only demonstrated acts of kindness toward you in the past. But even in absence of this conversation, you can have the confidence that there is likely a reasonable explanation for his current actions. This is the lighthouse principal and will guide you to shore and save your friendship.

What would happen if, when you do speak to him, he responds, "I thought we agreed that I would pay you back on the 23rd, not the 3rd." So by virtue of a simple misunderstanding, you were ready to cause real harm to your friendship instead of relying on what you know about the person from the past. If you used the baseline for what you know about the person's character and what they did in the past, that would provide more valuable guidance than trying to interpret a single incident on its own. Use what you do know to help you understand what you don't.

When I was in college, I used my girlfriend's car to get to classes and make business appointments as a budding entrepreneur. She was kind hearted and taught me a lot about caring for others. She usually got off between 6 and 8 p.m. depending on her shift and didn't need her car while at work.

She bought a car precisely because she did not want to rely on others for transportation. So, it was totally reasonable to expect that if she was kind enough to lend me her car, the least I could do is make sure she got to and from work on time. I always got there on time and would typically have to wait until she finished any last minute tasks before she was able to leave. One night, I wasn't.

I had a full day of classes and meetings and went home about four-ish. And while I didn't plan to, I fell asleep. This was during the days when phone booths were the norm and cellphones were something you read about in science magazines. When she got off from work and didn't see me, she waited for a while, then called me several times. I never heard the phone.

I was startled when my sister knocked on the door and I had no idea what time it was. She passed me the phone with my girlfriend on the other line. I picked up half asleep and was like, "Hey, what's up?" It was almost eight o'clock and we were supposed to be at a youth meeting at 7:30.

I think she was holding off on nuclear war, as she wanted to determine if something else had killed me first. Finding out, perhaps disappointingly, that I was alive and well, she unleashed her rage and dropped nonstop torpedoes before the phone conversation ended in a nuclear explosion. "You overslept? How could you oversleep? You left me stranded in the middle of nowhere, in the middle of the night, and I had to call for a ride! And you're in MY CAR!"

She was understandably upset given the circumstances. But here's the thing. I had dropped her off and picked her up a million times before, on time every time. My oversleeping wasn't a sign of disrespect or not caring, or not appreciating that she loaned me her car. My oversleeping only made me human.

In many ways throughout our relationship, she had a lot of evidence that showed I was someone that deeply cared about her well-being. This should have provided context to guide her disappointment and to prevent her from having to judge me through the lens of a single incident. But her anger got the best of her, clouded her judgment, hurt me in the process and just made for a very awkward situation for a while.

She was right to consider that there was a possibility I

could have been in an accident. But that was not the only possibility that could have explained why this happened. Now, in full disclosure, if the shoe were on the other foot, I probably would have acted the same way. But that does not mean that we should not handle situations like this more wisely.

If someone has consistently demonstrated they care for you and something happens which makes you question how much they value you, make sure you do the math. Check your human calculator because something here just doesn't add up. You may have ignored your baseline, which is the starting point to provide perspective.

My girlfriend had a baseline with a lot of data that should have guided her to consider if these accusations of irresponsibility and ungratefulness were true or warranted. They weren't. Interestingly, because I knew the type of person she was, it was easy for me to understand her position and to also forgive her outbursts as I started from the baseline of what I already knew about her to be true.

Friendships forged over a long time deserve the benefit of the doubt when an incident occurs that challenges the notion of the character of your friend. It should serve as your lighthouse to guide you to a better idea of what may really be going on.

Incidentally, a short while later the roles would be reversed. My girlfriend would no longer have a car, but I bought my first. She dropped me off to a friend and went to my apartment to rest and relax for a while and agreed to pick me up at 9 p.m. She didn't.

I never heard from her and had no way of reaching her, so at midnight my friend had to drive me home. When we got there, my car was sitting in the driveway safe and sound. Inside, she was sleeping like a baby and woke up startled and embarrassed.

There she was with my car and keys to my apartment while I was stranded by my friend's place. I guess I could have used that as an opportunity for revenge, but I knew she wasn't an irresponsible person. She was an angel, but with human tendencies.

12 Pot, Meet Kettle

Everyone is a hypocrite, and there is a reason you cannot see this.

On the evening news you hear a driver that knocked down a little child was found to have alcohol in his blood. Do you think he was irresponsible and should go to jail? Have you ever drunk at a party and then drove home afterwards? Maybe you don't drink, but have you ever texted while driving? It's the same level of irresponsibility.

Do you frown at the person who got caught stealing on the job but use reams of paper at work to photocopy your church bulletins? Or have you chosen not to reveal all of your purchases to a customs officer when returning from a trip? Any time you hear someone say, "Yes but the difference is..." then know that you probably just tuned into the hypocrisy channel.

Hypocrisy blocks empathy and is the greatest threat to friendships and to mankind. To be more specific, your hypocrisy is the greatest threat to your friendships and to your peace on Earth with others. We are all hypocrites. As soon as we recognize this, we will find our most compelling reason to forgive and accept others and ourselves. If you cannot see this truth, it is because the log is firmly planted in your eye.

In most cases we don't recognize that we commit the same acts we indignantly judge others for. Even when we recognize the similarity, we quickly use a lopsided justification scale that judges their acts to be far worse than our own.

We morally condemn others while putting the halo of justification on our own head. We turn up our nose in judgment of others, yet congested by the sinus of our own BS, we cannot smell the stench of our hypocrisy. Don't ask yourself if you do this; ask if you can *recognize* when you do. Try to recognize it more in yourself so that you are able to empathize with others and forgive others. This is the first step toward peace and understanding within yourself, your relationships and ultimately the world.

As a young child, I remember getting an Atari 2600 game console for Christmas. It was not possible to be happier; it just wasn't. I could play Pac-Man nonstop and without having to cough up quarters at the local game room. I would play for hours and hours, only stopping to eat or bathe under parental threat of lashes with a cat-o-nine tails.

I was the envy of all my friends in our neighborhood and even the older kids would crowd our doorstep to get an opportunity to play on this addictive gaming console. It was mine all mine and I coveted it and lavished in all the attention I got for having it.

One day my younger sister Terear asked to use my Atari. I refused. She really wanted to get in on the excitement and picked up the joystick so she could play. I became enraged. "No you can't!" My mom observed this spat and suggested that I give my sister a chance to play. "It's been on all day and it's getting hot!" I chided while unplugging everything and rolling up the cord, intent to not give her a chance. "Besides, I'm tired!"

To this day I don't understand why I was being so selfish and mean toward my own sister. I was her hero. It would not cost us anything, not even a quarter, to play it at home as I had done for so many hours. Perhaps I was foolishly thinking this is just a toy for boys, no girls allowed. Whatever my motivation, it was just wrong.

Although it seemed like days, it wasn't more than twenty minutes later that one of the older kids came to the door asking if we could play Pac-Man on my new Atari console. Without thinking twice about it, I said sure and excitedly unwrapped it and plugged it in. We jumped on the sofa in front of the TV, laughing and playing and having the time of our lives.

My mom heard the older kid at the door propositioning me to play, so she stood by to watch and see what I would do. When, without hesitation, I went to the console and set everything up and began playing, she was upset by my choice and chastised me. "Your sister was just begging you to spend five minutes on this gaming console, but you shouted at her and gave her every reason in the book that she couldn't play, and she's your blood! Then you have these friends showing up and you fall over yourself to let them play. And I hear you laughing and having a great time with these so-called friends, but you disrespected your own sister!"

I wasn't even twelve at the time. Her words rang to the core of my soul. I could not enjoy another moment of the game with my friend. Everything had changed as those words cut deep. I could smell the stench of my hypocrisy and it made me sick. Every time I think back at that moment, I want to throw up.

How could I have been so selfish? How could I have disrespected my own sister in this way? Why was I not able to give her five minutes of joy even after my parents bought me this console to bring me joy in abundance? Why did it not give me pleasure to think about being able to put a smile on my sister's face? Why was I so anxious to put a smile on my friend's face?

And the biggest question of all, how could I not see the double standard? This wasn't hours or days later. It was just minutes earlier that I had sworn three times that no one should be allowed to play my precious console. Then I heard the crowing of my mother's voice. I know just how the apostle Peter must have felt.

Elephants are not hypocritical because, unlike humans, they do not suffer from moral Alzheimer's. They have incredible memories. They can recall another elephant or human even after they have not seen them for years. If an elephant has met you before and meets one of your family members decades later, it can tell that you are related. After long journeys, they remember it forever due to their photographic-like memory.

Paradoxically, a human's memory is often very selective. This can lead to a holier-than-thou attitude, which is a breeding ground for hypocrisy and the potential to lose dear friends. In my small network of friends, we share money as a resource because funds are necessary to get so many things done but it is not always available. It's our way of protecting each other through life's experiences. It also makes sure we have the resources needed to take care of the curve balls that life is quite accustomed to throwing.

On one such occasion I requested funds from a close friend who responded by saying he couldn't lend because he had a very low risk tolerance. Despite what he may have intended, his words cut deep. There have been times where I had to help him out financially since the incident and even times when he forgot to or simply could not pay me back. During those times, the wound was still fresh and I wanted to remind him of those words. But I chose instead to use the baseline and history of our friendship to manage my reaction and to keep things in context.

I reminded myself that I had been the recipient of his kindness on many occasions without hesitation. It's important to have the memory of an elephant, lest you forget the kindness of a friend just because there was an incident where they did not react the way you wanted them to.

My friend Dwayne has an uncle in California that used to say, "Just live a while!" He used it every time he overheard someone judging the actions of another swearing they would never do the same in life. His response was always "Just live a while!", meaning that if you live long enough you will eventually witness people do things and commit mistakes you swore were impossible before.

If hypocrisy is the clothing of the unwise, then a rush to judgment is its tennis shoes. The hypocrite wrongly believes that if he hasn't committed a particular mistake before then he is somehow qualified to pass judgment on others. This rush to judgment is fraught with problems. If you have never experienced something, you are little qualified to speak on the matter.

I once witnessed an older lady act in disgust because her brother who suffers from Alzheimer's kept going out of the house and getting lost. When I tried to help get him back home, she quipped, "If he ever gets lost, don't call me, take him to the police. I'm so sick and tired of him. I'm older than he is and I don't do that foolishness!"

Her rush to judgment was in not understanding that her brother has an illness. He wasn't getting lost for giggles! My rush to judgment was in wanting to call her an ass, which I did (don't rush to judge me!). But on further reflection, I saw that the real problem was the enormous ignorance that still surrounds this devastating illness. We are all hypocritical at times and we all rush to judgment at times.

The point I want us to consider is that if we stretch our memories far back into our past or far enough into our futures, we would understand that at one point or another we have all been hypocrites. As such we should try to remember all aspects of our relationships with our friends. Don't rush to judge them because of something you cannot currently understand or your inability to make the connections between their faults and yours.

How many times have you done a favor for a friend where they don't seem willing to do the exact thing for you? Most people remember and hold on to that, become angry and resentful, and treat their friends differently. But we often forget how many times that same friend has given us a ride to work without asking for gas money. Or invited us to their home for great meals without charging even though it costs to feed your guests. Or loaned us books or DVDs over the years, which have a value in their own right.

Besides, if you're giving only when you expect it back, it's not really giving as much as it is a business transaction. I'm not saying that we should not expect things back when we lend, especially when we are specifically clear that we expect it back. What I am saying is that the truly remarkable giving in a friendship is when you do so without the expectation of receiving something in return, and you're still happy.

Don't play forget. Don't shortchange your friendship through a false sense of righteousness. Everyone will have a moment where they put their foot in their mouth and say something they regret, do something they regret, or be in a foul place momentarily. This makes us human.

But examine who your friends are on the whole and how you are with them on the whole. Just because your vice is not same as theirs, it doesn't make you better, just different.

When there's a problem between you and your friend, do you feel rage instead of compassion? Are you anxious to prove you were right instead of giving a nod to your friend's point of view? Do you feel like everyone commits mistakes but this time they really did something you would never do? Do you find yourself privately discussing the issue with everyone except your friend, even to the persons who you are normally not close with?

These are very high indicators you are probably being challenged by hypocrisy without realizing it. It happens to all of us. Realizing it is the first step in being able to put this great destroyer of precious friendships back in the box. This chapter is dedicated to your first step.

13 What The Flock!

A man is known by the company he keeps.
~ Euripides

My male friends are great dads. All of them. Sometimes I wonder if I subconsciously interviewed them, did a background check and had them pass a friendship exam before we could be certified friends. However, if they weren't great dads, we probably couldn't be friends because I couldn't respect that. Another thing I notice about my friends is that they are responsible and reliable. They are always looking to learn something new and are respected in their various circles of friends and associates. They work with purpose and stand out in their fields. I find this interesting because this coincidence was never planned. Or was it?

There is a popular saying "Show me your closest friends and I can tell you who you are." I can attest to this. We can tell so much about a person just by examining their friends. A related saying is "Your income is the average of that of your five closest friends." Sadly, in my case, this is also true. And if those buggers would only apply themselves more, I could really make it in life!

Choose your friends wisely. It's one of the most important decisions you will make in life. I've had times where I had to systematically disassociate with acquaintances who, upon closer examination, had character traits that I strongly disapproved of. We were going in completely opposite directions in life. If I started to become close with someone and discovered they were a drug user, involved in criminal activity, or abusive to those around them, I reexamined that relationship and put a lot of distance between us.

Don't get me wrong: we all need friends, but friendship is a choice. I choose to be friends with persons that share similar core values and character traits as I do, even with our individual human flaws. I have found this path to friendship to be more rewarding and filled with less regret.

If you wrestle with a fool, onlookers will not be able to tell the difference. If you are not proud of the life your friends live, if you don't aspire to be like them, if their character is filled with vices you disapprove of, you need new friends or the chances are great you will suffer their fate. If you got this far in the chapter and were wondering if I would use the saying "birds of a feather flock together," then wonder no more. Besides, it's true. You will find that rich people tend to flock with the rich, poor people with the poor, religious with the religious, and hookers with other hookers.

The point of this chapter is a simple one of examination. Look at yourself and your circle of friends to determine if you feel proud and blessed to be in the circle you are in. If you lament your situation and desire to have a different experience, then change your environment and identify the types of persons who are on paths you aspire to. Flock with them and you will become like them. It's as simple as that, even when it's not as easy as that.

14 Worry About Your Scripture

Few love to hear the sins they love to act.
~William Shakespeare

Have you ever noticed how much conflict has been caused in the name of religion? Of course you have. Wars between Christians and Muslims, Catholics and Anglicans, Baptists and Protestants and everything in between have been done in the name of Holy Scripture. Even within the same religion, you will find strife and conflict that each person says is based on scripture. Factions exist within the church, between husbands and wives, children and parents, and among neighbors. People battle each other and use their points of view to try and win an argument.

Sadly, no relationship is immune to this. A religious husband may tell his wife, "Honey, the Bible says 'wives obey your husbands.'" The wife may retort, "And the Bible says 'husbands love your wives as Christ loves the church and died for her.'" A parent may say, "Children, obey your parents," and "Spare the rod, spoil the child."

Their kids will likely fire back, "Parents, do not lead your children to anger."

If you believe this sort of battle is limited to religious circles, you would be mistaken. A girlfriend complains to her boyfriend, "You never buy me anything nice," to which he responds, "You never buy me anything, period!" In a conflict among friends, one says, "Why are you so late? You know I have to be to work on time!", while the other feels "I got out of bed early and was stuck in traffic for two hours, why can't you appreciate this effort?"

Many years ago, my friend Dwayne had unique advice for religious folk who were always excited to point out other people's flaws using the Bible as ammunition. "Worry about your own scripture!" he said. It was so simple, yet so profound.

Essentially, he meant, "If you were doing what you are supposed to be doing, this conflict might not exist. Be more concerned about that."

How often do we demand to be understood without trying to understand? How often do we accuse someone else of being unreasonable or unfair when we ourselves are doing the exact thing we are accusing them of? That's because we don't want to be fair: we want to win, at all costs.

Empathy is one of the most critical components of a successful friendship. We have to be able to put ourselves in someone else's shoes to begin to understand how they feel. Our actions and reactions should be guided in part by this.

I once had a neighbor who in my opinion wasn't very neighborly. Each week on garbage day she would ignore my bin when taking hers to the curbside. Both cans were side by side, behind the gate of the apartment complex, but each week she would only take hers to the front and leave mine.

If I saw them first, I would take both out to the curbside. If I got in first from work, I would return all empty bins to the place they were kept. But if she got in first, she would only take hers and leave my empty bin and the shared recycle bins. This went on for months. At first I thought it was completely random. Then I noticed that she was very consistent. I would take out and return both bins, but she would only take out and return hers.

For a while I continued to take out both bins because I wanted to show that as good neighbors we should help and look out for one another. It was like trying to teach a lesson to a can of paint.

This went on week after week for several months. I grew to resent her attitude. It was as if she was saying, "If you're stupid enough to take out my garbage even when I wouldn't touch yours, then I'm smart enough to let you. Dummy!"

So then I thought, okay, two can play this game. Though it wasn't my style and I didn't feel right doing it, I was upset and thought I'd teach her a lesson. One of two things would happen, I thought. Either she would learn her lesson or at least I'd stop looking like such an ass. I started doing what she did. I only took my garbage out even when they were both side by side. If I got home first, I would only retrieve my bin, leaving hers to the curb.

I did this for about three weeks straight, and do you know how I felt each week? I felt like crap. It just wasn't me. I wasn't comfortable trying to be a bad neighbor, nor was I able to be ambivalent about it. I'm just not built that way. Worse than the feeling of letting someone think they are using you was the feeling that I was participating in being an ugly, inconsiderate person, something I detest, and it felt horrible.

The best way to succeed in life is to act on the advice we give to others.
~Author Unknown

That's when I remembered my friend's words and I immediately recognized why I felt so bad. "Worry about your own scripture!" That was it. I was turning into someone I detested, and even worse, I was allowing someone else to cause me to do this. Why? Because I became too concerned about "their" scripture, "their" responsibilities.

It's known that you should never argue with a fool because he will bring you down to his level and then beat you with experience! You can't lose if you don't play their silly game.

Even among friends we can sometimes feel like we're being taken advantage of. We count how many times we picked up the tab during our last three outings. We feel like we're the ones always calling to check in on them but they never initiate a call to us. We're the ones complimenting them on how they look but they hardly return the favor.

We've loaned them things without hesitation, but they are hesitant when we ask for something. It's only natural to want to receive the love you perceive you give. We want to live in a world where everything seems fair, and of course no one wants to be made a fool. Be careful not to lose who you are in these moments.

Why do you actually do what you're doing? Do you call to check on your friends because you want them to call you, or do you do so because it's the right thing to do? Do you buy them coffee because you expect them to buy you coffee later? What if they never did? What if in ten years you were the only one that bought your friend a cup of coffee?

I say, great! Be who you are because of who you are. Worry about your own scripture, about your own behavior, about the things that make you, *you*. Do the right things for the right reasons. Give without expecting to receive. Give because it feels good, and because it's what you should do. If they return the favor, great! Extra blessings. If they don't, still great because you are being the best version of you that you can be, and not because of what you hope to gain in return.

I've found that among genuine friendships, being concerned with your own responsibilities and not trying to negotiate good behavior is a very rewarding experience. Believe it or not, it is also *the* best way to teach someone how they should behave. Sure, sometimes people tend to have the blinders on and may not immediately see the wonderful things you do, or recognize how they can grow in that area, but you're not doing it for that reason.

Sometimes when I want someone to understand a lesson but I don't want to create an unpleasant situation, I comment on it but in a positive way. I find an external example, as people tend not to be offended when they are not directly involved in a story. For instance, instead of complaining about not receiving a call from them, I express my happiness that I can tell they are always appreciative when I call them.

I may say, "I do this because of who I am, not because I'm looking for anything in return. I may call you ten times a month and you may not call me at all that month, but it's ok because it's what I want to do and I know you appreciate it." Many times, this is all that is necessary for them to consider they were often on the receiving end of kindness from a friend and it encourages them to return the favor. It may not be at a level that you do, but they respond because it resonated. Then your phone rings!

We do not all have the same gifts, and we do not always see the world the same way. Do not resent the fact that you do good for someone else, even if they don't return the favor. Do not worry about what they should be doing for you. Just do what you are supposed to do. When each person's actions are independently weighed or measured, at least you know that as a friend, for as much as it depended on you, your contributions will be valued because you did your part, and it wasn't conditional.

I once saw someone very dear to me get into a shouting match with their parent. It got ugly and almost became physical. As a witness I can tell you their parent was being extremely unreasonable and was the ringleader in the whole dispute, even to the point of physicality. But it's very important not to let others drag you down, not to allow them to force you to behave as they are behaving.

Were they justified in screaming back at their parent and their minor scuffle? They certainly had enough provocation. But they also had the opportunity to respect the position their parent had and to simply walk away. I say "simply," but that doesn't mean it would have been "easy." You need the presence of mind to want to do the right thing and to not allow others to dictate your behavior like I allowed my neighbor to dictate mine. However temporary, it was still personally disappointing.

Long after that incident, I still took out and returned her trash bin along with mine on garbage days. I did it because it was the right thing to do, it's who I aspire to be, and that's not dependent on the actions of another. Try it with this understanding. You'll feel better for it, I promise you.

15 When Friendships Are Derailed, Swallow Pride

Strength does not come from winning. Your struggles develop your strengths. When you go through hardships and decide not to surrender, that is strength.
~Arnold Schwarzenegger

When I was seven, I froze as I witnessed my father slap my mother with all the force of a domineering man. It was frightening like the collision of lightening and thunder and it paralyzed my younger sister and I. Although I had heard them arguing before, I had never witnessed any physical confrontation between them. To see a man, any man, lay his hands on your mother, is traumatizing at any age. For as long as I live I will never forget this day but perhaps not for the reasons you suspect.

My father is a mechanic. He works on car engines all day. His hands are huge and callused from all of that manual labor. When he hit my mother in the face, I heard the explosion of a cannon from a large warship. My world stood still from shock. Her whole face jerked from the impact as her head ricocheted to the right. It seemed like a bomb exploded beneath the surface of her cheek and the ripple effect spread in slow motion throughout the rest of her round face. I stood in the aftermath of this warzone explosion and the resulting look of horror and disbelief on her face mirrored mine.

As her head turned back toward my father, her eyes widened! I have never seen that look on her face before, or since. It wasn't a look of fear. It wasn't shock. It wasn't sadness. It was the purest form of indignation and rage I have ever seen in real life. My mom lost it. She went into the kitchen, pulled out the biggest knife she could find and returned to the living room, the scene of the original assault.

You have to understand this was not a violent household nor were we exposed to violence as a family. Sure, they argued from time to time, but it wasn't the order of the day. My father was not a violent man and he only hit me once in my entire life. He never spanked us; that was my mom's domain when we deserved it.

My mom is also not a violent person. She is in every sense of the word a lady, full of respect and love for those around her. Always. She always chooses a kind word to calm those who would seek troublesome means to resolve an issue and is known as the peacemaker and mother hen to hundreds of people. This woman has always been a Mother Teresa of sorts. But not on this night.

What happened next would be burned into my memory and my heart forever. My mother came back into the living room with a knife, enraged but not wild. She returned with this purposeful, singular focused anger. She was unpredictably dangerous while she held this Friday the 13th knife in her right hand that seemed the size of a machete. My father looked upon her trying to maintain his position of control and bossiness, but he was clearly confused, and like me, wasn't sure what the hell was going to happen next. She screamed and shouted out his name. And then it happened.

She marched within twelve inches of my father and dropped to her knees. I could still see the scene like a camera circling 360 degrees around her. She was a warrior like Leonidas in the movie *300* preparing for a final battle scene. She firmly gripped the knife in her right hand by the handle and began to beat her chest with a closed fist, the blade pointing down the whole time. You could hear her fist pounding on her chest with each pulsating strike as if to add validity to every word she was about to utter. The knife, primed for action depending on the reaction of her enemy. Then she shouted these words, which I will never forget. "Andre, you could do whatever you want in this life. But if you EVER and I mean if you EVER lay your hands on me again IN FRONT OF MY CHILDREN, as GOD is my witness this day, I will KILL YOU!"

There was no creature in heaven or Earth, alive or dead, in that room or in any corner of the universe that would have doubted her resolve or didn't believe her. My father immediately realized he was in clear and present danger. He was confused. He was afraid. He didn't know how to act. He tried to mutter an incoherent response while not making eye contact with her. He looked around for his keys and left.

To me, as a seven-year-old kid, that day was not marked as the day my father hit my mother. Instead, it was the day I realized how much my mother loved my sister and me. It was the day I realized she loved us more than life itself. The day I realized she would give her life or do whatever it takes to protect us, keep us safe and make sure we recognized we had a mother we could always, and I mean always, depend on and be proud of.

So why am I telling you all of this? In The Bahamas we have a saying "mouth can say anything." It's the equivalent of "talk is cheap." My mom could have simply told us she loved us more than anything in the world and would fight and die to protect us and keep us safe. That sounds great, but it is easy to say. Instead of talk, it is rather trials and actions that demonstrate and prove this to be true. It is only when we are tested that we know what we are made of. In fact, it's deeper than that. It is our tests and trials that actually make us.

Relationships are fortified by trials, by problems, by obstacles. We are bound by these experiences and they either fortify our bonds or reveal them as being too weak. Your struggles develop your strength. If she did not have that experience where she was tested, she would not know what she was made of. We would not have known. But as a result of that singular trial, we all knew, my dad included.

The same is true of real friendships. Every friendship,

like every relationship of consequence, is tested by at least one major conflict, and sometimes by several. It might be a verbal argument where regrettable things are said. It may be a conflict that ends in a physical fight. It might be the pain you observe in your partner after you cheat on them. It could even be that momentary thought of selfishness, greed or jealousy that causes you to make a decision against your friend that you later regret.

Sometimes they just catch you on a bad day when everything is going wrong and they happen to say the wrong thing at the wrong time. There are tons of opportunities to derail a friendship. I can think of at least one with each of my closest friends and without too much thought I can think of many others. But what do you do when conflict derails your friendship?

I have a friend – let's call him "Dominic" because, um, that's his real name. I met Dominic as a teenager in college and we've been friends ever since. We share a passion for knowledge, technology, and all things interesting. We value our moral standards, self confidence, personal pride and we are both observant to a fault. We have a tremendous amount of respect for each other and think our wits are Wyatt Earp fast. Incidentally, it would be some of these same characteristics that would cause the most devastating blow I have ever received in a friendship.

It was brutal. We fell out of favor with each other and anger and disappointment was all that appeared left. He saw me through lenses that suggested I was a person different than I was, and I resented to the core that this was what he saw.

Our pride and observational skills did not serve us well in this conflict. We believed what we believed, saw what we saw and to hell with any other point of view. There was no retreat, no surrender, just an all-out assault. I have never experienced this kind of distress or sense of loss as a result of a conflict between friends. And there weren't even any women involved! Just a lot of misunderstanding and a whole lot of pride.

Then there was the aftermath. We decided it was best that we just not be friends. By this time we had already been friends for more than fifteen years. It was tough. It was also hard to know what to do at that time. If you ever find yourself in a similar conflict with a good friend, I recommend three important tools: time, space, and a damn good calculator.

Why? Well, despite our human tendency to want to fix everything now, time is necessary to allow healing through perspective. There are things to consider that anger and immediate pain just do not allow entering into the equation. Have you ever tried to cook a lot of rice in a small pot? When the water boils, it tips the lid and spills into the fire, ruining everything. But if you use a big enough pot with sufficient space for the rice and water, in time the pressure will dissipate and you will end up with nice and fluffy rice.

The same is true for many conflicts. We need time and space to see things we can't see while we're upset. For Dominic and I, we needed enough time to sit back and look at the whole picture. We needed an opportunity to consider the past fifteen years, not just the past fifteen days. Then it was time to pull out that damned good calculator. A relationship calculator allows you to add up all the pluses and minuses of a friendship to see what its true value is in your life.

I highly recommend you use a calculator and not just make up numbers in your head. What do I mean by this? Well, how many fifteen-year-old friendships do you have? What has been the glue that held the friendship together during all of that time? Why were you friends in the first place? How many other friends do you have that bring that same level of value to your life? Persons you can talk to, depend on, rely on to keep your secrets, that share similar passions, and that can actually relate to the things you relate to? That's when you begin to realize how important and valuable that friendship is.

Sure, while you're angry and cooking under pressure with a small pot, you're liable to think "I don't care, I don't need that kind of friend in my life because they upset me. I'll just hang with my other friends." Then you realize the uniqueness of that friendship. The advice, the laughter, the sharing of experiences and the confidence that allowed you to fortify this friendship over all these years are what makes it valuable. Only an idiot would not value that. Only an idiot would not feel that sense of loss over time.

If, while getting out of your car, a penny fell out of your hand and under the car, what would you do? Most people would simply count it as a loss and walk away (with the exception of Mr. Burns from *The Simpsons*). But for most people, it's just not worth it. A penny is nothing. You will probably find three more of them just on your way inside the grocery store.

But what if that was a hundred dollar bill that fell out of your hand and underneath the car? You'd be on your hands and knees like a U.S. Marine crawling under barbed wire fences, through landmines, while scratching both elbows because hey, that's a hundred bucks, yo! It took you a much longer time to obtain it and it can do a whole lot more for you than a penny could, so you value it. At that point, pride becomes less important. What's more important is reuniting with Ben Franklin.

If a friendship is ever derailed by conflict, give it some time and space, count the cost of the friendship and then be the first to extend the olive branch. "I don't care who's right or wrong, I just value our friendship and hope we still have an opportunity to be friends" is a perfect way to begin the healing process.

It's like getting down on the ground for that $100. You will often find that your true friend is willing to join you on hands and knees as well to help find that c-note. Sometimes, things get so screwed up that we need a reminder about what the value of our friendships are, how difficult it is to find a true friend and how important it is to work to maintain that friendship.

The friendship that Dominic and I have has been fortified through that tremendous test of its value. It is absolutely stronger as a result and also serves as a guide for me with other friendships I have. Trials and challenges aren't just something that friendships survive; they fortify them and make their bonds unbreakable. I don't believe we ever actually apologized for our words or actions during that conflict. We were just smart enough to get down on the ground and search for our hundred-dollar bill, to swallow our pride and push that derailed train back on track. Our friendship has been going strong ever since.

16 Birthdays, Weddings and Funerals

We need a witness to our lives.
~ Susan Sarandon

Some people have a knack for remembering dates such as birthdays, weddings, anniversaries and funerals. I am not one of them. As a self proclaimed introvert, I've rarely attended such events and almost never remember these dates. I've always felt personally uncomfortable in these situations. Over the years, I've experienced a few things that have caused me to pivot on this point of view.

We need a witness to our lives. There's a billion people on the planet, what does any one life really mean? But in a marriage, you're promising to care about everything. The good things, the bad things, the terrible things, the mundane things, all of it, all of the time, every day. You're saying, "Your life will not go unnoticed because I will notice it. Your life will not go unwitnessed because I will be your witness." ~Susan Sarandon (in *Shall We Dance*)

My brilliant friend Felicity shared this quote with me.

I'm glad she did. Few things are as gratifying as finding a perfect explanation of a powerful emotion that was previously difficult to put into words. When that magical moment happens, it makes you want to say "THIS! This is the perfect way to describe how I feel!" The quote by Susan Sarandon regarding why relationships are so important perfectly captures and explains why.

I didn't always get it, but I've come to understand why it is so important to take note of special events in our friends' lives and celebrate it with them. It gives the moment significance. It says, "Your life will not go unnoticed, because I will notice it. It will not go unwitnessed because I will be your witness." That's why it is important to acknowledge and celebrate our friends' birthdays, weddings, funerals, graduations, bar mitzvahs, promotions, accomplishments, and everything in between.

I met Kess when I was four years old. He is my oldest friend in the world and occupies a place in my heart that is sacred. Kess was raised by his grandmother who we affectionately call "Rambo," 'nuff said. And his relationship with his mother Sandra matched the closeness of the relationship I have with my own mother. When Sandra passed away, he was devastated.

At Sandra's funeral, everyone that was close to me attended. They knew how much my friendship with Kess meant to me and wanted to show their support, even though most of them had never met Sandra. I'm not a fan of funerals and I've skipped many of them in my life, even ones that I should have attended in retrospect. I didn't think twice about attending Sandra's funeral. She was a kind-hearted soul and was this other cool mom that I had. I had known her all my life since I was four.

For years after Sandra's funeral, Kess would miss her and mourn her. He was living in the U.S. and Sandra passed away in The Bahamas. I would go by the gravesite from time to time to make sure the caretakers were doing a good job, keeping flowers there and sending an occasional photo to Kess, which he seemed to really appreciate.

Many times he would call me at strange hours of the morning. In tears. Telling me how much he missed his mom, and how much he appreciated that I attended the funeral. At first, I didn't think much of it. After all, he was my brother and she was like a mother to me, of course I would go. Then on some of the calls he would express his painful disappointment that some people he considered friends did not attend. You could tell it was far more pain than it was anger or disappointment. It was then that I realized that my justifications for not attending other people's special moments were not justified at all.

I used to think, "Hey, I really didn't know your cousin like that" or "I'm not going to enjoy this birthday party because I don't know anyone there I can talk to or relate to, so why should I go?" Kess made me realize two important things. Firstly, it was not about me! Those events didn't exist for my pleasure or enjoyment. They weren't there so I could rate them out of five stars on how beneficial they were to me. It had nothing to do with me. It was about my friends. They needed me at this time. They would really appreciate if I could be there.

Secondly, our friends need us to notice and bear witness to their lives so they know that in a world of more than seven billion people, their lives actually matter to someone, someone that matters to them. That's our role as friends, to show that their lives matter. However insignificant their promotion, graduation, birthday, funeral is to other people, they need to know that it matters to us. Through this act of kindness and love we show them they are not alone in the universe.

Many years later I attended the funeral for the mother of another close friend, my partner in crime, Roper. Drucilla Roper, my friend's mom, was easily one of the most delightful persons I have ever met. Any time I think about her, I immediately see the big yellow sun smiling on a box of Kellogg's Raisin Bran. She just represented a giddy joy and kindness of spirit to me. So I could only imagine what she meant to Roper. To say they were close is like saying Siamese twins are sort of connected. When she died, he cried, and so did I.

At her funeral, it struck me that even though she had a strong representation from all the people that she knew, I didn't notice any of Roper's friends, particularly those that he and I had in common. I remember him walking up to me at the funeral, heart heavy, he looked me in the eye and said, "Thanks for coming, man, I really appreciate this."

Even though he spoke those words with his lips, I could tell they originated from a deeper place. It's a feeling I'll always remember. He was going through tremendous emotions of loss and grief and I was there to support him. I wanted to let him know that her life and what she meant to him will not go unnoticed. I was there to bear witness as his friend and help to mark and solidify the importance of this moment in his life. That's what friends do. That's why we are here. That's why it matters.

I've only had two birthday parties. Once when I was eight years old, my mom had a birthday party for me at McDonalds. I still remember the striped Le Tigre shirt I had on and the Gold Digger blue jeans with zipper pockets (I thought I told you not to judge me!). All of my friends were there: Obinna, Kess and my first girlfriend Erica. It was awesome. I still have the photos. The whole world stopped that day to recognize my existence and it made me feel special.

As someone that never felt comfortable in social circles, I remember opting not to go to many weddings, funerals and birthdays. So it was surprising to me that some twenty-five years later I decided to have another party. It was the first time I invited friends to an event that I was hosting and I was really afraid that no one would show. Perhaps it would be some sort of payback for all of the times I missed in the lives of others that I cared about. What happened was absolutely incredible and unforgettable. Practically all of my friends showed up. It was an incredible moment to see so many people take time out of their busy lives to pause and mark this day with me and celebrate in my honor. I felt privileged.

I was thirty-three at the time. Out of the hundreds of people that showed up, there were two people in particular that made the night unforgettable for me. My dear friend Richard and his beautiful wife Ruth attended. Despite having thirty more birthdays than I had, Mr. D, as I like to call him, has become one of my most respected friends. He occupies the role of friend, confidant, father, trusted advisor, mentor, brother and a host of other roles that could not fit in this book. He's seen it all and done it all, twice. Dignitary, politician, millionaire, ambassador, hosted and been hosted by kings, queens and presidents, orphans and paupers.

All of this is great, yet means nothing. What does mean something is that he is a man among men with a genuine heart. His sole purpose in life is the uplifting of every human being he meets and the preparation of a better way for those who would come behind him. I felt honored that he and Ruth, herself a woman among women, would take the time to mark this occasion with me.

I mentioned all of this to say that their attendance at my birthday party, along with all of my other friends, made it a day I will remember for as long as I live. This is what friends do. They make your life mean something through this recognition of friendship. It has changed how I view my role in my friend's lives.

Do you know why men build monuments? We build monuments to honor those people and events that have had a profound affect on us. We build them so we never forget. We construct them so that we can revisit them and relive those moments and mark them in the annals of time. As a kid I remember a poem on my grandmother's wall that said "God gave us memories so we could have roses in December." I didn't understand what the poet meant at the time. But later I came to understand that our memories let us relive great experiences after the moment has passed, even when those we care about are not with us.

When we join with our friends to celebrate their triumphs or walk beside them during their trials, we build a memorial with them to mark the event and make it special, to make it matter. We honor them. For all the weddings I've subsequently attended, all of the baby christenings, birthday parties, funerals, dinner invites, graduations and anything that those we love hold dear, I now realize the reason I do this. I also have a new appreciation for any time my friends pause their lives to help me celebrate mine.

We don't have forever, we only have right now. It's easy to get lost as one person in a planet of billions. The feeling of insignificance, of being just a number, just a statistic, that you matter to no one, is incredible, overwhelming and sad. Take the time to show those you love that what's most important is not that they matter to the whole world. What's most important is that they matter to you. Their lives will not go unnoticed because you will be their witness.

17 I Trust You With My Lotto Ticket

Trust is confidence without evidence.

You will be hard pressed to find a greater gift in life than when a friend grants you his trust. It is a sacred thing. Imagine someone winning the lotto and showing up at your doorstep to say, "You are the only one I could trust, please keep this ticket safe for me." No man is an island. At some point we need to share our burdens and triumphs. We are blessed when we can find a friend who will allow us to reveal ourselves and not judge us or use it against us. This is the Holy Grail of friendship.

Even in the criminal world, where honor is rare, they hate the very idea of a rat. This is someone who has been entrusted to keep a shared vulnerability secret, but instead chooses to reveal it in a way that will hurt those involved. As human beings, this is how much we value trust and show disdain for those who betray it.

One day while I was still living with my parents, I rushed out of the house and left a private but opened letter on my bed. Realizing later what had happened, I called my mom and said, "I need you to do me a favor. I left a very personal letter on my bed and I would like to trust you to secure it for me. This is important to me so please don't read it, but put it away in my drawer."

I know that curiosity normally gets the best of us, but I had faith in my relationship with my mom that she would do the right thing in this circumstance. If she ignored my request and read the letter, it would have been very embarrassing for a friend of mine that entrusted it to me. I would also have been embarrassed as the person it was entrusted to. I never worried about it after asking my mom to secure it and to not invade my privacy. She would later tell me on a few occasions how proud she was of that moment. She was proud that I had entrusted her with such a personal task and in such a confident way. She was also proud of herself for living up to that trust.

Nells, as I like to call her, often jokes that she was itching and burning to read the letter, only because I said it was top secret, of course. But she realized what was at stake and was proud of herself for not doing so and for the way our relationship was strengthened as a result. This is how you build trust.

I've seen many action movies where the bad guy has cornered the good guy's friend and threatens to torture him unless he reveals his friend's whereabouts. I often wonder what I would do in that situation knowing they will hurt my friend or worse if they find out where they are. I guess if it's Tamico they're asking about, I'd probably give him up in two shakes of lambs tail! He tried to leave me behind on a vacation trip to Honduras; clearly he's no marine. But if it was Kimwood, I'd try and hold out, at least for fifteen minutes, because the man makes the best pancakes I've ever tasted on this side of the Atlantic and they're free.

Bob Marley once sang, "Only your best friend knows your secret, so only he could reveal it." When our friends confide in us, we have to remember that we have been chosen as trustworthy to protect what they hold dear. It is an honor and a privilege. Words cannot describe the comfort this gives to the soul who entrusts themselves to you. This is true for keeping private information in confidence and to coming through for friends that depend on you.

My mom used to tell me growing up that the problem with sharing your vulnerabilities with someone and hoping they will keep it secret is that everybody has two best friends. She meant that when you share your private challenges with Sam, he'd share it with Tom. But Tom is close with Jim and shares your secret with him. You get the point. So, Bob Marley was right. Again.

Sometimes I wonder if Nells knows just how wise she is. When she shared this with me as a young child, it encouraged me to live up to the standard to which my friends were entrusting me. If they confided in me, then that was for my ears alone, not for me and my other close friends.

Though we often think that gossiping is the domain of women, men prove that women don't have a monopoly on this. People talk. In the movies I'll notice that a guy often takes the intimate things he hears from his buddy, especially relationship woes, and shares it with his girlfriend, because they "share everything."

I notice that girls do the same thing too. As if our partners get this automatic exempt pass and end up learning things about our friends they were not intended to know. Think about this the next time you are sharing stories in bed. A good rule of thumb is, if you would be embarrassed to let your friend know that you shared his or her confidential information with someone else, including your partner, then don't share it.

In high school, a close girl friend once shared with me how she lost her virginity on the beach. The very next day we met in the same class and were talking about something totally different. At this point a mutual friend walked up to her and said, "Hey, have you ever had sex on the beach?" with this huge naughty grin on her face. I crapped my pants!

My friend immediately turned to me, her eyes wide, her face red. She pinched me and her mouth stretched open. She was flabbergasted that I would share such an intimate story she told me in complete confidence just one day earlier. Except I didn't! I was just as shocked and felt I was in the Twilight Zone. How could this mutual friend know this? It seemed obvious that I had to have told her. Even I began to wonder if she used some kind of brain scan on me.

As it turned out, it was neither. This mutual friend had just been out that weekend and was introduced to a new drink at the bar called, you guessed it, "sex on the beach." She was so thrilled by this party discovery she wanted to immediately share it. Fortunately enough, my friend was too shocked and stunned to mutter, "How could you tell her what I told you!" She and I laughed about it later, but for a minute there I wanted to be in China. If you are from China and you just read that last sentence, I guess that would not make any sense to you. Just think of it more like "I wanted to be in America," assuming this conveys the same idea of being as far away as possible.

I'm not upset that you lied to me, I'm upset that from now on I can't believe you.
~ Friedrich Nietzsche

Nietzsche had it right. In other words, what really bothers me is not only that you betrayed my confidence, but that I no longer have a special friend with whom I can confide. This represents a tremendous loss and helps to underline why it is so important to earn and keep our friends' trust.

Even though I've emphasized the idea of being a trusted confidant, we earn trust in many ways. Trust is built when our friends know that we always, always, always have their best interests at heart. Knowing that we're always in their corner, making sure they're ok, and that we would never do anything to deliberately hurt them, is something that builds enormous trust and mutual respect between friends. This is something more valuable than silver and gold, and though some of my friends will disagree, even more valuable than football season tickets.

18 The 7-Digit Spirit Boosters

A word of encouragement during a failure is worth more than an hour of praise after success.
   ~Author Unknown

At one point or another, I've seen my closest friends at the end of their rope, hanging on by a thread. Heart heavy as lead, grasping for air, for a reason to go on living as life kicked them in the balls or ovaries. We've all been there. If you haven't experienced it yet, just give it time.

Yet these are the most positive, well-adjusted people I know. I've seen my friends fall apart watching their marriages disintegrate right in front of their eyes. Some have attempted to commit suicide while others have lost everything and ended up homeless. Sometimes our world falls apart, sometimes we're just having a bad day, but we all need someone to check in on us from time to time. It can literally save us.

One day I was working in a top floor office building

downtown and could see a friend walking past below. She always dresses nicely, is very positive and it's always a pleasure to talk to her. I called her cellphone and told her I was watching her every move and to be careful crossing the street. She seemed astonished by my extraterrestrial powers. I went down to say hello, but she didn't make it past three sentences when out of the blue she just burst into tears. She was in a desperate financial state and felt overwhelmed by the bills and the bank calls and the stress.

I was only calling to say hi, but the call was timely. As we spoke, I reminded her that she had many good options and that although this seemed overwhelming, to stand back, breathe and rethink the options she had available to address her major concerns. She did, and at the end of the conversation she felt encouraged that she had what was necessary to deal with the financial and psychological challenges in front of her. She left with a little more pep in her step. That's the power of picking up the phone and checking in with your friend. You never know what someone is going through, and you never know how much they may need a word of encouragement.

With some friends we hardly initiate contact; we just sit back and wait to receive. Even if this doesn't bother your friend who mostly calls you, it's still a fantastic idea to reach out from time to time just to see how they are doing. You can dial seven digits and lift their spirits.

I have another friend I'm so close to that I can tell how she is doing from the first word she utters. It's all in the way she says "hey," and I pay attention. When she's in pain, I feel it. She's had a lot to deal with, more than it's fair to ask a small village to bear, yet she's had to bear it alone. We all have our dark days. We all have our moments when we feel alone. We won't always reach out, and sometimes we need our friends to reach in.

My friend Peter was born in 1921. That's a long time to gather a lot of wisdom, and apparently a lot of humor. Whenever I call to check in on him, he always thanks me for calling in the most genuine way. Sometimes I get so caught up in work and special projects that I don't get a chance to spend as much time with him as I'd like. I always enjoy our chats and so does he.

Peter once told me that only the good die young so I had no need to worry, as I'd probably live to be one hundred and fifty. I'm still not sure how I should feel about that! I remember being surprised to find out that he still gets depressed or upset. I know it sounds silly, but at ninety-two and retired I guess I thought he had it made in the shade. But we're all just human. We're all just trying to figure life out. Sometimes, even during our lowest of lows, the voice of a friend can lift our spirits and rest it on Mount Everest so we can catch a second wind. Don't take the idea of your friend's well-being for granted. Check in.

19 3 a.m. Comfort

See that light down the road, it's goin' guide you there
Two sets of footsteps, I was right beside you there.

-But what about them times I only saw one?
-Those were the times that I was under the gun,

It was then I carried you, my son.

~ DMX, "The Convo"

During the 2008 democratic race for the party nominee of the U.S. presidential election, Barack Obama and Hillary Clinton squared off in one of the most interesting political races of modern time. One intriguing aspect of the race was the strategy of the Clinton campaign to pitch her as the more experienced candidate who could be counted on as president in the time of crisis.

It was dubbed the 3 a.m. phone call moment. What would happen if in the middle of the night catastrophe struck and the president had to be called in. What would Barack Obama do if he got that 3 a.m. phone call? What would Hillary do? It was a strategy designed to address confidence, comfort and security.

Even late night talk shows and *SNL* got into the game. In one particular scene on *Saturday Night Live*, Obama is seen calling Clinton in a panic, to which she retorts, "Man up, Barack!" Though the scene was funny, they were also onto something. Nothing makes us feel more secure and comforted than knowing when the chips are down (what does that mean anyway?) we can call our friends with confidence knowing that they have our backs.

It's perhaps more than anything else the litmus test we use to qualify our "real" friends.

They are friends we can call at a moment's notice, day or night, with all the confidence in the world. Unquestionably and without hesitation, we know that they will help us. And if they don't have all the answers, they will help us look for the answers.

A friend and I have a running joke about a phone we call the BAT phone. Any time, day or night, if we send out a signal by calling the BAT phone, we know that our superhero friend will be there to respond, no exceptions. Besides the obvious Batman reference, it was a term also used at my company for when a customer called our main line. After three rings, an old bell phone would ring loudly in the center of the office. When it did, you knew it was critical, that a customer was having difficulty getting through, and now the boss had been alerted, so you Better Answer That phone. So we called it the BAT phone.

A few chapters back, I talked about the significance of my thirty-third birthday and how I had the most awesome party ever. All of my friends were there and I was the host with the most. When my good buddy Dwayne left the party, most of us were still there. To give you some perspective, Dwayne is the big brother I never had and my truest confidant. Sure, he pisses me off too, but his friendship means more to me than winning the world's biggest jackpot, if only by a hair. He called me about fifteen minutes after leaving the party to say he had just crashed his car.

When I got that call I was trying to reconcile a lot of things in a few short seconds. I had only just seen him and he was fine. Now he was saying he was in a big accident. He sounded fine. Then he said the car was "gone" and that the ambulance was on its way. A drunk driver had broadsided him and the car was totaled and he was pretty banged up.

That's when I realized the gravity of what had happened and that it wasn't a fender bender. If you know Dwayne, you know he doesn't like to be a bother, even to his own self. So if he's reaching out, something big is happening.

I had to leave my party, all my friends, family, guests, the food and the live band and rush out to see how I could help my friend in need. And not just for his sake. My world would be very different if anything ever happened to him. His friendship just makes being alive and taking this journey that much easier, more interesting, more valuable, more fun.

He told me not to call his wife, who happens to also be my cousin. He didn't want to worry her. After the paramedics strapped him in and put him in the ambulance, I followed them to the hospital. A long night. Police got involved. Thankfully no broken bones. Of course the drunk driver wasn't insured, that would make too much sense.

While it wasn't quite 3 a.m. when he called, I could tell what level of comfort he got knowing that he could reach out to me. I was having the time of my life, hosting the party of my dreams, with dignitaries, friends, family and acquaintances, attending in my honor. But he knew that I would drop it all in a heartbeat if he needed me.

- Black and white debonair Kangol hat, $85.
- Live band playing the coolest Caribbean hits all night, $2000.
- Brand new Toyota that's just been written off, $40,000.
- Knowing that, day or night, no matter where, when or how, your friend would drop everything in an instant if you were ever in trouble, priceless.

Imagine you had to blow up a huge yellow balloon the size of an airplane. Then, after expending all your energy to blow it up, someone comes along and sticks a pin in it. Pfffftt! You feel the air gushing out and watch it deflate right before your eyes. When we make that 3 a.m. call on the BAT phone, desperate and distraught, it only takes a careless response from a friend to stick in a pin in your balloon and totally deflate your spirit.

After struggling to resolve the problem on our own, we are often in a fragile state when we make that call. We fight back pride and blow ourselves up like that big party balloon just to have enough courage to reach out to a friend and expose our weakness.

At times, because of pride, we try to mask the seriousness of the situation or our desperation. Our friends may not pick up on this and their nonchalant response pierces our spirit and clips our wings. On occasion they may not detect our cues or perhaps are going through a difficult moment themselves. As a result, they don't pick up on the critical nature of the call or our fragility and desperation while reaching out for help.

Try to notice this in your friends. If they are calling and asking you things like "Hey, are you busy?" or "Did I wake you, sorry to call you so late," pay attention that you're not being dismissive. The scar of that rejection, especially when they really need you, can last a lifetime.

I had a girlfriend that taught me how to love and how to recognize love. She taught me so much and meant the world to me. One thing I always remembered was the fact that I could literally call her 24-7/365 and she would always make me feel like, hey it's ok, I'm here to listen if you need me. Amazingly, she was like that even if she was upset with me.

Now, I know what you're thinking. How could anyone ever be upset with me? I'm a sweetheart. Yeah, but that's because you've obviously never dated me. Even if I were the cause of her pain or anger, she would always take my call. At 3 p.m. or 3 a.m., wide awake or deep in sleep, alone or surrounded by thousands, she would always take my call. She was always willing to lend an ear or help me if she could. For this friendship, I am eternally grateful.

When James Gandolfini, the actor who played Tony Soprano on *The Sopranos* passed away, many people came forward to pay tribute. I remember John Travolta's tribute the most. Travolta recalled that when he tragically lost his son he was inconsolable. He was at his home in Florida and filled with grief.

He said that Gandolfini, his friend of many years, called to check on him incessantly. He also said that Gandolfini, who was in much demand as an actor, stopped everything, came down to see him in Florida and said he would not leave until Travolta was better. Gandolfini said he would stay as long as his friend needed him to.

The power of love in that friendship touched me just hearing John Travolta recall that story. I could only imagine how it touched him in his darkest hour. Having someone in your life to respond to your 3 a.m. call is one of the most precious gifts you can have.

"Dude, I don't know if I'm gonna make this, man! Can you come down here?" That was the cry of a good friend of mine. He called me at work, and he was distraught. Although my friend was depressed and felt like he was dying inside, I couldn't just drive over. He lived in another country and it wasn't that easy.

I had just started my own company and life as an entrepreneur was kicking my butt: so many responsibilities and challenges and so little money. Of course I couldn't just stop everything, put my company in jeopardy and fly over there. It would have been reckless, irresponsible and unprofessional.

So after my flight landed, we embraced and I knew I was doing the only thing I could do. Over the next few days we would talk and talk. He would have an opportunity to process what he was going through, get some much-needed encouragement and rethink what he thought was an insurmountable situation. Above it all, he was just so glad that I came. That act alone provided a level of comfort and appreciation that he would remind me of for years to come. He would always reflect on it and tell me how much that act of friendship meant to him.

When we're in despair, though fragile like that big yellow balloon, we are at the same time triumphantly positioned to fly again. We just need a gentle breeze underneath us to push us forward. We get this second wind from the encouragement of a friend responding to our 3 a.m. call. They are always willing to catch us when we fall and blow a gentle breeze our way to lift us up through acts of friendship. I like to call this gentle breeze hope.

20 Who The Hell Is Kess Anyway?

All differences in this world are of degree, and not of kind, because oneness is the secret of everything.
~Swami Vivekananda

I was never a Houston Rockets basketball fan. I don't know how to play American football and I don't follow the sport. I'm not particularly superstitious and I don't give conspiracy theories the time of day. Strip clubs were not a favorite past time for me in my early twenties and I don't wear basketball jerseys as an official form of casual dress. I was never fascinated by gold chains, and I do believe that there are other beautiful women in the world besides Latino women. But my friend Kess is the exact opposite. Friendships come in all shapes and sizes and it's our similarities that help us to understand and respect our differences.

Much like a Venn diagram, there are several areas that all my friends can relate to, but outside of that, they could not be more different. A hard concept for some people to grasp is that we all have multiple personalities.

A woman may have to fight to find balance between being a wife, and a mother, an aunt and an engineer, a democrat and a closet artist. We can't be boxed in and put into nice neat piles.

Our friendships are similarly diverse. Though there is often a common thread of trust and respect, the difference between our friends' characters can be stark. We shouldn't be made to feel there is anything wrong with this. My friend Mel has the purest intellectual technology mind of anyone I have ever met. We could literally spend days discussing binary digits. But he would feel like a fish out of water at a Willis and The Illest concert with my friend Dominic, who also happens to have a technology background.

I've never met anyone who shares my love for clever rap lyrics at the level Kess does. It's not something that I could share unequivocally with the rest of my buddies. Years ago I remember giving an IT director of a Radisson Hotel a ride to pick up his vehicle from the repair shop. We had spent a lot of time talking over the years throughout various IT projects. These were the days of MP3 CDs and I had one of my usual mixes in the car. A Wu Tang joint, followed by Queen's "Bohemian Rhapsody," then came a Marc Anthony hit with the reggae dub star Bounty Killer in tow. I remember Clayton looking at me like I was an alien. "What is this mix of music you are listening to? I had no idea, I would have never guessed it."

I think about this whenever I find myself scratching my head at the type of buddies some of my friends have. I would see someone I have a lot of intellectual conversations with spending a few hours talking to one of their friends. Just listening in makes me think this is what waterboarding torture must feel like. Surely. That's when I realize that you and I can be good friends, but I may have other friends that you cannot relate to and vice versa.

So I totally get it as Kess scratches his head when he considers some of my other friendships. This makes me realize just how unique each of our friendships are and how we cannot simply replace one person with another as friendships are not about body counts, despite what Facebook would have us believe. They are all unique and special in their own way and our recognition of this helps prevent us from trying to make it what it isn't.

I met Kess when I was four years old and we've been friends, more like brothers, ever since. Our bond is unbreakable, yet we've never had a lot of mutual friends. I realize that's ok. I realize that we are unique human beings and each of us, even though we may have lots in common, are attracted to different things and that's a good thing. It gives us more perspective and more to share. So don't sweat it when some of your friends can't relate to other friends you have. We don't all like spicy foods, we don't all like pizza, we don't all like Asian cuisines, but I couldn't imagine a world without all this wonderful and necessary variety.

21 Saying Goodbye Without Knowing It

It's so hard to say goodbye to yesterday.
~ Boyz II Men

Growing old together isn't something we dream about only with our spouses and partners. We also like to think we will grow old with our friends.

Motivational speaker Bob Proctor once held up an hourglass and put his hand over the top half. The only thing visible was the tiny center where you could see the sand falling and the bottom part of the glass where all the sand fell. It was a powerful visual to illustrate the point that we never know how much time we have left in our lives. The top part is always covered. We only know what has happened in the past, which is the bottom half of the glass and what is happening right now, which is the sand falling. Do we have one grain or thousands of grains left?

Bob went on to give two examples. He said he remembered his sixty-year-old grandmother constantly telling them that she was getting old and probably didn't have much time left. She said that for years and at one point he says jokingly, "We loved her but we thought she was never going to die." She actually lived to be ninety-four. At the same time he recounts that when he was a kid, he had a friend named Bob Yates. Yates had an accident on a bridge and lost his life at sixteen. Bob said if you had asked Yates how much time he thought he had left he would have said at least a quarter of a century, but he didn't even have a minute left. We never know how much sand is left in the top half of the glass. So we should value this time, be mindful of how we decide to spend it, and think about this as we spend time with family and friends.

Earlier this year I got a call from my good friend Stephen. He wanted to know when I would be in town again because he wanted me to meet his estranged daughter. He was so proud to finally be able to try to construct a meaningful relationship with her and wanted her to get an opportunity to meet his friends. I believe he wanted her to get a better insight into the type of person he was. I told him I'd be in town soon and looked forward to it. That was the last conversation I would have with Steve before his life was taken senselessly.

We had so many wonderful times together as friends and I will never forget him. I used to think we would grow old together and just talk and laugh about all the crazy things we did and all the jokes that had become classics. But in that phone conversation I said goodbye to my friend without even knowing it. His birthday is in this very month of October as I write this, but for the first time he won't be around to celebrate it.

There is an important lesson here. Make time for your friends. Find out how they are doing. Take them up on their offer to have coffee with you. If you find yourself canceling multiple times on planned get-togethers, stop it and go. Avoid senseless arguments and strive to keep the peace. Every encounter with your buddy could be your last encounter with them. What would your life be like if they weren't in it? Who can you count on as your real confidant? There is always a possibility that you are saying goodbye without knowing it.

Nos vemos mañana si Dios quiere. That's Spanish for we'll see each other tomorrow, Lord willing. There are many folks who say the same thing in English. The strange thing is that we are creatures of habit and patterns. An experience that was originally unique and exciting loses its luster over time as we repeat the experience.

Think about when you first learned how to drive. Grown ups would say sure you're excited to drive now because you're just learning, but the time will come when you will hate to get behind the wheel. Of course we couldn't see that. We just saw how sweet it was to finally have the independence to drive and how our social status would skyrocket as a result. But after too many trips on the road our perspective changes and we look for ways to avoid the road and traffic.

That's the challenge we have as we try to remind ourselves about the frailty of life. When you see someone like Bob Proctor's grandmother living to be ninety-four, you start to feel like we're all going to live to grow very old. But like Bob's friend Yates and my friend Stephen, every life comes with its own hidden expiry date.

That's why we celebrate birthdays, anniversaries and other special occasions. If you are really wise, you have learned to celebrate each day in the same way. Stephen's passing made me realize just why we should celebrate birthdays. Every time we make it to another one, it's a gift and at that point, we don't know if we will make it to the next one.

As is often the case in tragic situations like Steve's unexpected passing, surviving friends and family members often grapple with feelings of doubt regarding whether they could have done something to prevent what was destined to happen. We also struggle wondering if our friends realized how much we loved them before they died.

I am confident that Steve knew he was my brother and I loved him dearly. I know he shared the same feelings toward me and our friendship. It's the one thing that comforts me. Even though we said goodbye without realizing it, we always took time to honor our friendship. This brings comfort, even in sad moments like this, and that's a good thing.

I wrote this book to let you know you've already won the lotto and you're sitting on millions. If you have one true friend, even with no money in the bank, you are richer than you think. Reflect on the things we have talked about and use these tools to help navigate the most precious relationships you will ever have.

As long as you have real friends, you will always be rich, you will always be blessed. As long as you continue to be a real friend, you will always make others rich, you will always be a blessing to others.

Share these thoughts with your friends because sometimes we say goodbye without knowing it. Sometimes without warning, things just come to an end.

ABOUT THE AUTHOR

Born in Nassau, Bahamas in 1972, Duran Price is an entrepreneur and author of *The Opposite Of Poverty Is Friendship*. He studied Business & Information Technology at The College of The Bahamas and has always been fascinated by human relationships and what motivates us to feel and behave the way we do. A perceptive listener and thoughtful communicator, he shares his insights in ways that inspire and motivate his audiences.

Duran is an advocate for peace through understanding and empathy. He focuses on positive and thought provoking themes in his public speaking, books, music and blog projects. He taught himself Spanish which he speaks fluently, and is in love with Latin American culture.

Duran lives in Ontario, Canada and travels frequently throughout North and Latin America, The Caribbean and   Europe.

He can be contacted by email: dp@duranprice.com

If you found this book useful please help others discover this positive message by leaving a review on our website and joining the conversation at www.duranprice.com

Made in the USA
Lexington, KY
28 March 2014